Retire on Less Than You Think

Retire on Less Than You Think

The New York Times
GUIDE TO PLANNING
YOUR FINANCIAL FUTURE

FRED BROCK

TIMES BOOKS
HENRY HOLT AND COMPANY | NEW YORK

Times Books
Henry Holt and Company, LLC
Publishers since 1866
115 West 18th Street
New York, New York 10011

Henry Holt® is a registered trademark of
Henry Holt and Company, LLC.

Library of Congress Cataloging-in-Publication Data
Brock, Fred.
    Retire on less than you think : the New York times guide to planning your financial future /
    Fred Brock.
        p. cm.
    ISBN 0-8050-7374-4
    1. Finance, Personal—United States. 2. Retirement—United States—Planning. I. New
York times. II. Title.
HG179.B7438 2004
332.024'014—dc22   2003060149

Henry Holt books are available for special promotions and
premiums. For details contact: Director, Special Markets.

First Edition 2004

Designed by Kelly S. Too
Illustrations designed by Pat Lyons

Printed in the United States of America
10 9 8 7 6 5 4 3 2 1

contents

This book is a natural outgrowth of the "Seniority" column I have written for nearly six years for the *New York Times*'s Sunday "Money & Business" section. Writing the column and the book has been an engaging process of learning and discovery, the results of which I hope will help people focus more clearly on some of the big issues they will face as they plan their retirement. For most of us the main question is "Can I afford to retire?" On this central question, there is an incredible disconnect between the everyday reality of how much money it takes to live in retirement and how much money Wall Street and the mutual fund industry tell us we need. Unfortunately the media for the most part has blithely accepted the inflated projections of financial services industry "experts." This misinformation has created a lot of needless worry for many people, sometimes causing them to delay retiring. I hope this book will balance these self-serving projections and help people realize that retirement, however they define it, is not just a dream.

The book is intended neither as an investment guide nor as a self-improvement guide—except in the sense that your personal situation might be improved by retiring.

When calculating future earnings on savings, I have usually used a rate of 6.5 percent. I selected it because it seemed a middle ground between those optimists who see stock returns of 12 to 15 percent and the doomsayers who see 2 percent or less. Also, many very sober economists see market returns of 5 to 7 percent over the next decade or so. With online calculators, readers can easily substitute their own rate.

Because of the lag time in book publishing, some figures cited may be slightly out of date. But in most cases it's the relative differences between sets of figures that are important; they will most likely remain constant.

All the people described in these pages are real—with one exception. James McCain is not the real name of the retired professor in chapter 2. He requested that I not use his name or other details that would identify him, in order to protect his privacy. I agreed because, ultimately, his story is more compelling than who he is. Everything else about him, including the information on his personal finances, is accurate.

My first "Seniority" column was published in October 1998, at the behest of Jim Schachter. It was a profile of Elton Pasea, the "happiest guy in Texas" in chapter 2. It generated an initial heavy response from readers and confirmed Jim's sense that there was a ready audience for such a column. Many readers have since said that they like "Seniority" because it covers issues that affect their lives, and that they feel increasingly isolated from America's youth-obsessed media, especially television. They also have said that they like reading about the retirement experiences of others as a guide for their own plans and aspirations.

From the beginning, one thing came through loud and clear from readers: the concept of retirement is changing, especially among the baby boomers. Increasingly, life is viewed as a continuum and the divisions between work and recreation—and between work and retirement—are crumbling. Retirement is becoming a time not when we stop work, but when we work at what we love—on our own terms.

I am indebted to many people who graciously provided help and information when I needed it: Jeff Brown, Ken Dychtwald, Ann Fishman, Deena Katz, Richard Mayer, Ken Scholen, Bert Sperling, Fred Waddell, Tom Wetzel, Mark Weisbrot, and Stephen L. Wyss, to name a few. I am grateful to the people in the Social Security press office who always found answers to my questions quickly and completely. And, of course, I want to thank those people around the country, like Bill and Donna Taaffe, who allowed me to interview them about their personal financial lives. Some, like the Taaffes and James McCain, I interviewed exclusively for the book; others have previously appeared in the "Seniority" column.

I would especially like to thank Glenn Kramon and Jim Schachter of the *New York Times* for their support of the "Seniority" column; Judy Dobrzynski, who during her tenure as editor of "Money & Business" always made suggestions that improved my work; and the *Times*'s Dan Cooreman, whose wonderful headlines added an extra dimension to the column.

I will always be grateful to my wife, Evelyn, for her help in organizing and editing the manuscript.

Finally, thanks to Elton Pasea. He showed the way.

Retire on Less Than You Think

1

Do You Really Want to Retire?

In the twentieth century, we gained an additional thirty years of life.
It took the preceding fifty centuries to do that. That's extraordinary.
— ROBERT N. BUTLER, M.D., PRESIDENT,
INTERNATIONAL LONGEVITY CENTER-USA

The basic idea behind this book is simple and straightforward: you can retire sooner and on less money than you think, and live quite well, if you are willing to make a few relatively painless lifestyle changes.

A 2002 poll in *USA Today* on Americans' financial wishes showed that 62 percent dream of early retirement. But an AARP poll later that same year found that 77 percent of fifty-to-seventy-year-old investors had lost money in the stock market over the previous two years; of those who had losses, 21 percent said that they had postponed retirement as a result. In a 2003 poll cosponsored by the Employee Benefit Research Institute, 24 percent of workers forty-five or older said they planned to postpone retirement because of shrinking investments.

This is a book for the dreamers who want to retire sooner rather than later but are afraid they can't afford it: people who yearn for the time to realize a lifelong dream or avocation; people who have reached a dead end in their careers or who are burned out after years of doing the same thing and want to move on; or people who simply want a change. It is also for those who are at or past the traditional retirement age of sixty-five, but continue to work because they are convinced they don't have enough money to retire.

Also, of course, it is for those who suddenly find themselves involuntarily retiring early because of employer cutbacks. Such forced retirements usually involve so-called incentive packages that may include a lump-sum payment or extra years credited to your retirement account—or both. Many forced retirees are equally apprehensive, perhaps even more so, about whether they can afford retirement.

SMOKE AND MIRRORS

Whatever the situation, most people are victims of "data" circulated by the financial services industry—mutual fund companies, stockbrokerage firms, and banks—which hold that you need at least 70 to 80 percent of your preretirement income in order to retire without becoming a charity case. This figure has become conventional wisdom and is routinely and endlessly repeated in newspapers and magazines and on radio and television shows that offer financial advice. Little wonder people have come to believe it. It has struck fear into the hearts of baby boomers, who are known for spending, not saving.

There's only one problem: it's not true!

Worse, people in the financial services industry know it's not true. It is clever advertising bait to lure investors.

In the April 2003 issue of *Money* magazine, the columnist Jean Sherman Chatzky looks at a hypothetical twenty-four-year-old earning $35,000 a year and making a 10 percent contribution to his

401(k) plan. She assumes he will face annual inflation of 3 percent, annual salary increases of 6 percent, investment returns of 8 percent during his working years, and 5 percent during his retirement. By age fifty, he'll be making $150,000 a year and have $500,000 in his 401(k). By fifty-nine and a half, when he can withdraw 401(k) money with no penalty, his balance will be $1.24 million.

Chatzky then concludes that he will require $177,650 a year to retire, based on the assumption that he will need 70 percent of his preretirement salary. At this rate, even with Social Security, he will have drained his 401(k) dry by his sixty-ninth birthday! Chatzky's solution: save more and work longer. She says not a word about reducing expenses.

If you sense there is something wrong with this picture, you're right.

SOUL-SEARCHING

Retire on Less Than You Think will clear away the smoke and mirrors from retirement planning and show you that, in fact, you probably can retire much earlier than you thought.

Before you start calculating how much you will need to retire and what sacrifices you must make to do so, you should first do some soul-searching. Decide if you really do want to retire and what you will do with your newfound freedom. Where will you live? What about your friends and social life? People often talk glibly about how much they look forward to retirement, without giving enough thought and planning to the consequences of a major life change that can prove very disturbing and unsettling for those who are not psychologically prepared. Because people are living longer, retirement can stretch on for decades. If you retire at sixty and live to be ninety, you will have spent a third of your life in retirement! That can be a long time if you're just drifting and doing nothing. We all know relatives or acquaintances who retired and found themselves feeling bored and useless. I'm convinced that just such a situation contributed to the death of one of my uncles. After a long, busy career as a civil engineer, he just couldn't cope with lots of unstructured leisure time; for him it was far more stressful than working.

Ilene Cohen is the director of psychology at Bellevue Hospital in Manhattan and for twelve years was the senior psychologist in the hospital's geriatrics outpatient clinic. She regularly deals with people, especially men, who have difficulty with retirement. Men, she says, are more prone to defining themselves by their careers. "If your sense of power is defined by your job, retirement changes that," she said.

Paul C. Mims, who retired from a life of teaching English and art history in a Philadelphia suburb when he was fifty-eight, had to work through many of these problems on his own. When he retired, his first impression was that he had become invisible. "The minute I announced I was going to retire, it was as if I was no longer there," Mims said. "The same feeling continued for a while after I retired. I was no longer in the loop. That feeling of invisibility lasted until I got a new identity and got involved in a different kind of world." He now devotes more time to painting and does volunteer work at two museums near his home.

Manhattan resident Dan Cuff retired in 1999, when he was sixty-five, after working for nearly thirty years as an editor at the *New York Times*. He expected his wife—a social worker at a high school in the Bronx—would retire within a year or two. But things did not go exactly as he had planned. Because of the effects of the souring economy on the couple's investments, his wife postponed her retirement, leaving Cuff a bit adrift. As a result, he returned to the *Times* on a part-time basis about a year or so into his retirement. He says if he had it to do over again he would have continued working for another five years.

"Retirement seemed like a great idea at the time," he said. "My savings seemed pretty good and I thought my wife would retire soon. It wasn't really a tough decision; I sort of looked forward to it, to a break from getting up and working every day and getting on the subway and all that.

"But in retrospect, it might not have been the right decision. Even though you have a lot of freedom in retirement, you also have to have things to do. To fill up a day sometimes is hard, especially with my wife still working. Some retirees travel all the time, but we can't do that. I have a few things I do, like jogging and messing around on the computer. In the boom times I used to spend a lot of time checking on our investments. Now I don't want to see them.

"When you're thinking about retirement, you think that if you don't do it you might be dead in two years. But I'm still pretty healthy. I should have just hung in there, I guess."

Working part-time seems to suit him. "I was lucky to be able to do that," he said. "I still have a lot of free time." He and his wife have a house in the Berkshires in Massachusetts, where they go nearly every other weekend. He sometimes stays there by himself for a few days at a time. He says the problems he has had with retirement have been mainly psychological, but he is quick to cite what he calls the "financial component." "Our investments, and the income from them, have shrunk," he said. "It's not debilitating, but you have to think ahead. What if I live twenty more years? Will the money last? I guess it's the same stuff everybody worries about."

COSTS VERSUS BENEFITS

Part of the problem that people like Paul Mims and Dan Cuff encounter may simply lie in the word *retire*. According to my *Random House Webster's College Dictionary*, the first five meanings of the word are: (1) to withdraw or go away to a place of privacy, shelter, or seclusion; (2) to go to bed; (3) to give up or withdraw from an office, occupation, or career, usually because of age; (4) to fall back or retreat, as from battle; and (5) to withdraw from view.

Notice the emphasis on the idea of withdrawing, retreating, or giving up. No wonder retirement is sometimes viewed, and lived, negatively. But that outdated definition in no way describes many current and most future retirees. And it certainly doesn't describe the attitudes of baby boomers, the oldest of whom are facing retirement decisions.

Clearly another term is needed to describe this period of our lives, whether *third age, phase, stage, chapter*, or something else that reflects today's reality. Increasingly, those in this phase aren't about to withdraw, retreat, or give up. More about this later.

The move to this next phase of your life should be based on positive factors, not negatives ones: Retire "to" something rather than "from" something. Retiring simply to flee a situation you don't like can sometimes be an invitation to trouble. On the other hand, retiring in order to have the time and freedom to do something that you have always wanted to do—your second act, so to speak—is highly likely to have a positive outcome. You may even want to continue working, but in a different job or in a field in which you've always been interested but that perhaps didn't pay enough to raise a family or send children to college. Some people may not be able to retire for perfectly valid financial reasons, although I suspect that under closer examination many of these reasons might be greatly diminished.

If you have health problems, for example, and you have no retiree health benefits and aren't eligible for Medicare, you may be forced to keep working until you are sixty-five because of the difficulty and expense of buying an individual health insurance policy. The problem may not be insurmountable and is examined in detail in chapter 6.

If you are caring for an aging parent or parents, that financial burden could cause you to postpone retirement. The same can be true if you have an older child who has moved back home because of financial problems or you are contemplating a divorce that could greatly diminish your assets. Many baby boomers who postponed childbearing may find the expense of sending children to college conflicting with their retirement plans.

Other people, workaholics among them, may never want to retire because they are in love with, or obsessed by, their jobs. Still others have their personal identities tied up with their jobs and can't separate the two, like the men Ilene Cohen mentioned. Then there are those people who continue to work, even if they are unhappy, because they refuse to make even the smallest material sacrifice in order to jump off the labor merry-go-round. A workaholic executive once told a reporter who was interviewing him that he hated the weekends because he couldn't be at the office working. He said he wished he could just go from Friday right to Monday! We all know people who, while not classic workaholics, identify with their jobs so closely that they don't have much of a life outside the office or workplace. This is not a good omen for retirement. Then there's the woman who told me: "I would like to retire, but I won't do it unless I can live exactly as I live now. I don't want to give up anything." She may be missing an opportunity to open new doors and expand her horizons. For people in these situations— or some combination—early retirement may not be the best idea.

However, for most people there comes a time when they want to make a change and move on to another stage of life, much like a caterpillar becomes a butterfly. When that time comes, it is important that you be both flexible and proactive, that you find a way to make it happen. You need to do a costs-benefits analysis. On one side of the ledger are the benefits, mainly freedom and time to fulfill your dreams and desires. On the other side are the costs, mainly a change in lifestyle that will allow you to afford retirement. If the benefits outweigh the costs, go for it!

BACK TO THE FUTURE

First, a little history.

Ken Dychtwald, a well-known gerontologist and speaker who has written ten age-related books, including (with Joe Flower) *Age Wave: How the Most Important Trend of Our Time Will*

Change Our Future (J. P. Tarcher, 1989), likes to remind people that retirement is a very modern concept. "Most of us assume retirement is a given, an entitled period of leisure that's been around forever," he said in the course of several personal interviews. "That's just not true. In fact, today's retirees are, in many ways, a generation of guinea pigs. They're the first generation of men and women to be living long and retiring young, and attempting to find satisfaction in what has been promoted as this wondrous period, these 'golden years.'"

In fact, he points out, the concept of formal retirement didn't really exist before around 1900. "People weren't craving retirement," he said. "Work was seen not only as a way to provide a living, but a way for people to feel a sense of self-worth. It was an enormously potent engine of socialization, a way for people to stay in touch with other people of all interests and generations.

"Retirement as an institution emerged in the 1920s and really got traction in the 1930s, primarily because of the emerging field of management science and the belief that productivity was the engine that drove capitalism. And productivity, now that we were in a new industrial age, largely had to do with time and motion.

"All the early studies showed that if you were young and strong and quick, you were a valuable piece of the productivity engine. But if you were older and slower, it was a different story. So there was a rising feeling that older people should really be removed from the workforce.

"During the Depression when the unemployment level rose to more than 25 percent, President Roosevelt did a brilliant thing. He created the institution of Social Security whereby two problems could be solved. Older, less productive people could be removed from the workforce—thus boosting productivity—and younger people could be given a shot at a job and a chance to earn a living and start a family."

Although Social Security was signed into law in 1935, the first payments of monthly benefits didn't begin until 1940. The first person to receive a monthly Social Security check was a retired legal secretary, Ida Mae Fuller, of Ludlow, Vermont. Her check was for $22.54. She died in 1975 at the age of one hundred; during her thirty-five years as a beneficiary, she received more than $22,000 in benefits. In 1940, the government paid monthly benefits to 222,488 retirees for a total cost of $35 million. In 2002, 46 million people collected Social Security retirement benefits totaling almost $454 billion.

Those early days of a formal retirement system for workers were very different from what we see now. Even though Social Security benefits were available at 65, the average age of retirement in 1940 was 70. However, the average life expectancy then was 62.9 years—60.8 for men and 65.2 for women. Today the average age for retirement is 62 and in 2001 the average life expectancy was 77.2 years—74.4 for men and 79.8 for women. "People back then did not want to retire," Dychtwald said. "They bucked it. Not only did most people not want to retire; most didn't live long enough to do so. Those who did retire only had a few years. Retirement was believed to be a brief period of respite from a life of toil."

What happened to bring us to our current state, in which retirement is seen as another, productive stage of life rather than a short period of rest from life's toil before death? Two factors changed the retirement picture: increased life expectancy and rising affluence. We didn't get to our current situation from the 1930s directly. Social Security benefits were increased by Congress for the first time in 1950, by 77 percent. Between 1950 and 1972, benefits were increased only when Congress enacted special legislation, which it did every few years, usually in response to political pressure. Then in 1972 Congress raised benefits another 22 percent and provided for continuing annual cost-of-living increases linked to the rate of inflation. In the 1960s and 1970s, retirees were becoming wealthier not only through government programs like Social Security, but from bigger company pensions.

By 1960, the average life span had risen to 69.7 years (66.6 for men and 73.1 for women), and by 1975 it was 72.6 years (68.8 for men and 76.6 for women). It was this two-decade period starting around 1960 that gave rise to the idea of retirement as "golden years" of leisure. "The concept of retirement morphed somewhere around the 1960s and 1970s, the era in which most of us have grown up," Dychtwald said. "We began to glamorize retirement. We began to suggest that retirement, in and of itself, was heaven on earth. Work was the unappealing dimension of life; retirement and leisure were the treasures. Before we knew it, we had people clamoring for retirement. Leisure retirement became a mark of success, and the earlier you retired the more successful you were. If you bumped into someone at the airport and they said they were retired at fifty-one, you would believe them to be incredibly successful. That's the era in which many of us have lived. Unfortunately, most people have come to believe that's the standard and that's what everybody should try to do. But that's not what everybody wants to do. And that's not going to make everybody happy in their maturity."

Right now, he and many other experts argue, we are in the midst of another huge, even revolutionary, change in how retirement is viewed. This is in large part because of the 70 million or so baby boomers who were born between 1946 and 1964 and are starting to leave the workforce. They have remade the face of American life as they have moved through and dominated the demographic pipeline. They are doing the same for retirement. According to various surveys, including one by the AARP, 80 to 85 percent of the boomers plan to continue working, at least part-time, after they retire.

The word *retire*, which went from connoting respite from toil in the 1930s to a life of leisure in the 1960s, is changing again. "Yes, the dictionary says retirement means to withdraw or retreat," Dychtwald said. "But that's not how people are using the word now. We are discarding one model of retirement and embracing another. People see it as a period of engagement, of being involved and pursuing new dreams. There is a sense of self-determination. People now talk about freedom more than security, freedom from the burden of childrearing and the freedom of being far enough along in their careers to embark on new paths. There is a lot of talk about starting over rather than winding down or retreating. That is a big change. Many people now say, 'Retire is something old people do. I don't have any intention of being old. I'm not going to retire.' Retirement means the end of work, but everybody's talking about wanting to work." Clearly, he added, a new definition of retirement is emerging.

All this, of course, does not mean that people will continue on with the same careers or jobs. It does mean that they view retirement as another career or another job rather than a time of idleness.

It also means that a lot of retirement planners and so-called experts are passing out advice based on an outdated model of retirement.

Want a look at the "new" retirement? Warning: what you see may change your behavior. A 2002 study of retirees by Harris Interactive and Dychtwald has identified four main types of retirees— what they call the "four faces of retirement"—based on experiences, attitudes, and lifestyles. The study was sponsored by AIG Sun-America, a financial services company that is a subsidiary of American International Group. The survey—which was based on telephone interviews with 1,003 people fifty-five and older—also confirmed that traditional notions of what retirement means are pretty much out the window. "Not only is the meaning of 'retire' changing, even the language of retirement is changing," Dychtwald said. "People no longer talk about not working or taking it easy; they talk about 'reinventing' themselves and 'new begin-

nings,' of continuing to be productive but on their own terms."
Here are the four categories of retirees found in the survey:

- Ageless Explorers. These retirees represent 27 percent of those
  surveyed and are the leaders in creating a new definition of
  retirement. They see themselves in an exciting new phase of life
  and would rather be too busy than risk being bored. They have
  the highest level of education and have saved an average of
  twenty-four years for retirement.
- Comfortably Contents. This group (19 percent) seeks to live the
  traditional retirement life of leisure; its members aren't as interested in work or contributing to society. They have saved for an
  average of twenty-three years and spend their time on travel or
  other recreational activities.
- Live for Todays. These retirees (22 percent) aspire to be Ageless
  Explorers and may be even more interested in personal growth
  and reinvention than the actual Ageless Explorers, but they have
  always focused on the present and didn't devote much time to
  retirement planning. Having saved for only eighteen years, they
  have a great deal of anxiety about their finances and are likely to
  continue working in retirement in order to make ends meet.
- Sick and Tireds. This is the largest (32 percent) of the four
  groups and its members are in the worst circumstances. They are
  less educated, have fewer financial resources, and have low
  expectations for the future. They are more likely to have been
  forced into retirement by poor health and are less likely to travel,
  participate in community events, or tap into their potential. They
  have saved for an average of just sixteen years.

The survey was based on lifestyle and attitude questions, with
queries about incomes and net worth added only after the categories were established. "This was not a money-driven study,"
Dychtwald said. "We weren't looking for who's rich and who's
poor. We wanted to know how people are living this segment of

their lives. And these four categories rose out of the study like volcanic islands in the Pacific." The study is a strong indicator of the importance of planning for retirement, no matter how much money you make.

Michelle O'Neill, vice president of strategic consulting for Harris Interactive, the parent of the Harris Poll, said that the detailed questions in the survey indicated that "the happiness of people in these categories was not necessarily linked to how much money they had made or had; rather, happiness was linked with feeling financially prepared for whatever retirement lifestyle they wanted."

The study also points to the value of cutting expenses in order to meet retirement goals. Dychtwald noted that the Live for Todays often had made a lot of money and had a lot of good times, but lived beyond their means and didn't plan sufficiently for retirement. "They are financially vulnerable, and that's no fun," he said. "The Sick and Tireds are the largest and most unsettling of the groups," he continued. "Many were dealt a bad hand in that they or someone in their family is ill. They are pessimistic; for many of them, life is a wasteland that holds little promise of security, optimism, hope, or adventure. But some of their problems could have been helped by planning, which they did the least of, despite the fact that their incomes may have been lower or their education less. Long-term care insurance and more savings would have helped, for instance. It's hard to know which came first. Were they sick and poor and that put them into their present situation? Or were they people who had no vision or dream for the retirement stage of their lives and didn't prepare financially or psychologically?" He added that the Live for Todays and the Sick and Tireds—which make up 54 percent of the total retirees in the study—ought to be a wake-up call for the spend-a-lot-save-a-little baby boomers.

Jay S. Wintrob, the chief executive of AIG SunAmerica, agrees. He called the study a blueprint for future retirees and a "look at what's in store for the boomers." His company, however, didn't help pay for this study for purely altruistic reasons. It will use the survey's results as a tool to help sell its retirement services. Wintrob said he was surprised by the study because of his preconceived notion that the more money you had, the happier you'd be in retirement. "But we found that those who planned the longest were more prepared for retirement," he said, echoing O'Neill of Harris Interactive. "They were happier because their expectations were met."

The study put it this way: "While it would appear that money is the key to satisfaction, the research found that there is a stronger correlation between [satisfaction and] length of time saving and preparing for retirement—regardless of net worth." The study showed, for example, that 75 percent of those with "high financial preparedness" were "extremely satisfied" with retirement. That dropped to 46 percent for those with average preparedness and 26 percent for those with low preparedness. A further breakdown of the data showed that 61 percent of retirees who had saved and planned for retirement for more than twenty-five years were "extremely satisfied." That percentage fell to 51 for those who had saved for fifteen to twenty-four years and to 46 percent for those who had saved for fewer than fifteen years.

Looking even deeper into the results of the study is instructive. For instance, under the category of steps taken to prepare for retirement, 73 percent of Ageless Explorers had contributed to an individual retirement account, or IRA. This percentage fell to 68 percent for Comfortably Contents, 40 percent for Live for Todays, and 24 percent for the Sick and Tireds. As to who had purchased long-term care insurance: Ageless Explorers, 36 percent; Comfortably Contents, 42 percent; Live for Todays, 29 percent; and Sick and Tireds, 21 percent.

As to things they would have changed about preparing for retirement, 49 percent of Ageless Explorers would have started saving earlier, and 45 percent would have saved more; for the Comfortably Contents, the percentages were 54 and 57; Live for

Todays, 84 and 79; and Sick and Tireds, 70 and 66. Note that within each group, the percentages are very close for saving earlier and saving more, a further hint of the importance of planning.

"You can have somebody sitting on a pile of $100 million but having a miserable time of it," Dychtwald said. "And you can have a very happy teacher who's been putting aside a hundred dollars a week, who has conceived a dream for retirement that involves, say, some combination of leisure, volunteerism, and work that hits the balance for him or her perfectly. Such a person thought through a plan and gave consideration to the risks and obstacles, and believes the plan can handle them—that was the gem of the whole study. More critical than simply accumulating piles of money is taking time to create a plan. And not just a financial plan but a plan for a new life, for the rest of your life. The plan should be both attractive and doable. Some people dream of plans that are not realistic. It is important to take time over many years to develop a realistic plan and see it work. It is important to think about what you want to do, craft a plan for it, and have the financial elements in place for that plan."

Dychtwald says that an indication of how attitudes toward retirement have changed is that twenty years ago most people would have wanted to be among the Comfortably Contents. "That was yesterday's model: on vacation twelve months of the year," he said. "Now I'll bet most would identify with the Ageless Explorers. People now want more. A life of pure leisure is just not enough—socially, financially, or intellectually." But it takes planning to get there. "It's one thing if you're an Ageless Explorer and want to work because you find it stimulating and fun," Dychtwald said. "It's another if you're bagging groceries because you have to pay the bills."

After establishing the four categories of retirees, the survey then turned to money. Not surprisingly, those who had planned for retirement the longest had the most money. But answers to survey questions showed that it was a plan and making it work, not the amount of money, that spelled satisfaction.

The Ageless Explorers have an average postretirement household income of $64,800—compared with the overall national average of about $45,000—and an average net worth of $469,800; 75 percent have an investment strategy and a wide range of investments, and 60 percent received assistance in developing investment plans.

The Comfortably Contents' average income is $61,200 and average net worth is $367,500; 68 percent have an investment strategy and a wide range of investments, while 47 percent received assistance with their investment plans.

The Live for Todays have an average income of $46,300 and average net worth is $222,600; 51 percent have an investment strategy and a moderate range of investments, and 38 percent received assistance in developing an investment plan.

The Sick and Tireds' average income is $31,900 and average net worth is $161,200. Only 27 percent have an investment strategy and their range of investments is narrow; just 22 percent received assistance in developing an investment plan.

An important lesson in all this is that becoming an Ageless Explorer is linked more to your state of mind than your bank account. As this book will show, the group's average household income of $64,800 is not the price of admission. After all, the Ageless Explorers, the Comfortably Contents, and the Live for Todays all have household incomes that exceed the overall national average. For many people, satisfaction stems more from attitude than money. "Statistics on how much you need to retire are very dangerous," Jay Wintrob of AIG SunAmerica said. "Every individual circumstance is different."

Deena Katz, an independent financial adviser and the president of Evensky, Brown & Katz in Coral Gables, Florida, agrees. "Everybody loves rules of thumb, the press particularly," she said. "But I don't buy those rules of thumb."

THE BABY BOOMERS: THE ELEPHANT IN THE ROOM

Ken Dychtwald's observations that the meaning of retirement is changing and that more and more people refuse to think of themselves as old point to trends that will become very clear as members of the affluent, 70 million–strong baby-boomer generation begin to retire. Boomers are turning fifty at the rate of seven every minute and will continue to do so until 2014, according to *American Demographics* magazine.

In 2000, Harris Interactive conducted a broad survey for the National Council on the Aging on the "myths and realities of aging." It was designed as a follow-up survey to one done in 1974. The latest study clearly showed an increased feeling of optimism about growing old when compared with the 1974 data. Here are some of the findings:

- 84 percent of the three thousand adults, ages eighteen to eighty, who were surveyed said they would be happy if they lived to be ninety years old.
- 88 percent of those sixty-five and older said that when they looked back on their lives they were generally satisfied.
- 39 percent of the eighteen to eighty group viewed poor health as a very serious problem for older people; in the 1974 survey, it was 51 percent. "The overwhelming message is that Americans have discovered that getting older is not something to fear and that today's seniors are active, vital contributors to society," said a spokesman for Pfizer, which helped pay for the study.
- Nearly half of those sixty-five and older considered themselves to be middle-aged or young. Only 15 percent of people over seventy-five considered themselves "very old."

The survey also showed that retirement is increasingly viewed as a process, not an event—and that work and retirement are no longer mutually exclusive. Good health was considered more important than wealth by wide margins. Despite the general optimism in the survey, there were some concerns: 64 percent of all respondents were worried about losing their memory, and 59 percent were concerned about being denied medical treatments because of age. The effects of these changing attitudes and the approaching tsunami of boomer retirees—along with rising longevity—on our politics and culture will be staggering. "In the twentieth century, we gained an additional thirty years of life," noted Robert N. Butler, president of the International Longevity Center-USA. "It took the preceding fifty centuries to do that. That's extraordinary."

The "Repositioning" Generation

Deena Katz, the financial adviser in Coral Gables, Florida, is a fifty-four-year-old baby boomer with some definite opinions about her generation. She says the fundamental difference between boomers and their parents is in the boomers' philosophy of and approach to "things." "The big issue for baby boomers," she said, "is that they live in the immediate now. They have always given themselves everything they thought they were entitled to. When my folks needed a refrigerator, they saved money and bought it. Notice I said *needed*, not wanted. Now, when boomers *want* a refrigerator, they buy it and pay it off over time. So the boomers are absolutely going to have a hard time making an adjustment to a downsized lifestyle because they haven't saved enough to continue as they have been living."

But many will have to make that adjustment, and she expects the boomers to solve the problem in a way typical of their generation: they will change the rules. "I don't think the boomers will be a generation of traditional retirees," she said. "We will be a generation of repositioning." *Repositioning* is, of course, another way of saying that the boomers are going to continue working in some fashion and staying very active in their version of *retirement*—as has been indicated in most surveys.

But what about this generation's resistance to giving up "things" and living a less expensive life? "They are going to have to make some sacrifices and changes," Katz said. "And that will work for them if they are convinced these changes are positive rather than negative." She also thinks that a lot of boomers and others who say they don't want to move to a less expensive part of the country when they retire will actually do so when the time comes. "We'll see a great exodus from the cities into a simpler, less complicated lifestyle," she said. "But it will be a positive thing for the boomers: not 'You're going to have to sacrifice and downsize!' but 'I want to make my life simpler and the plus in that is that it's going to cost me less.' This will be their salvation from the problem of not having saved enough. When the mutual fund industry says you can't retire on less than seventy percent of your preretirement income, the boomers will say, 'Not me, baby; I'm going to figure it out.' The boomers will give panache to this new life. We're a time-poor generation, and the reward for this coming positive embrace of a simpler lifestyle is time and freedom and money. Saving money is like earning money."

So, basically, Katz thinks the boomers are going to avoid the train wreck predicted by the mutual fund industry and its 70 percent barrier by simply moving to another track. "All along the boomers have controlled the culture, as they will control retirement," she said. "They are redesigning retirement to accommodate what they lack, which is a strong financial base."

An April 2003 survey by Harris Interactive for Del Webb, the big builder of retirement communities, appeared to support Katz's observations. In the survey, 59 percent of baby boomers between the ages of 44 and 56 said they would relocate in retirement; in a similar survey in 1990, only 31 percent of those between 48 and 52 said they would do so. Of those planning to move, 31 percent expect to end up more than three hours' driving time from their current location. Those who planned to move to another state preferred Florida by 21 percent; Arizona, 18 percent; North Carolina, 10 percent; South Carolina, 10 percent; Tennessee, 9 percent; Colorado, 7 percent; Texas, 7 percent; Virginia, 7 percent; California, 6 percent; and New Mexico, 6 percent.

Where the Money Is

Katz's observations also are supported by a 2002 survey by Allstate Financial. Among other things, it found that 86 percent of baby boomers plan to spend as much time with activities in retirement as they do with work. About 60 percent think the best years of their lives will come after retirement. Many political observers think the boomers will use their numbers, and the resulting political clout, to force Congress to pass more entitlement programs for the elderly or improve existing ones. Perhaps. But right now the potential influence of these elder boomers is most evident in the advertising business, whether with advertisers who "get it" or those who don't.

Theodore Roszak, the author of *America the Wise: The Longevity Revolution and the True Wealth of Nations* (Houghton Mifflin, 1998), suggests that corporate America and its media are at war with the Census Bureau. "The young are a vanishing breed," he has written. "The future lies with the old."

While war may be too strong a metaphor and the young aren't really about to vanish, there is little doubt that the advertising industry has generally been well behind the curve of America's changing demographic landscape. Consider the following facts about this country's older population:

- People over fifty have half the nation's disposable income; 43 percent of new cars are bought by people in this group.
- Those over sixty-five enjoy twice the discretionary income of people twenty-five to thirty-four.

- The total net worth of people over fifty is five times that of other Americans; in the 1990s, the net worth of households headed by people over sixty grew 30 percent—double the national average.
- People over fifty account for 75 percent of the nation's financial assets and 80 percent of its savings and loan accounts.

As the boomers age, these numbers will become even more skewed toward older groups.

So what's going on? Why haven't youth-obsessed advertisers taken a cue from Willie Sutton, the bank robber who said he robbed banks "because that's where the money is." Nothing strikes fear in the heart of a television executive more than learning that one of his or her shows is attracting older viewers. The reason for this fixation on youth may lie in the demographics of the advertising business itself, where many decisions are made by people in their twenties and thirties who have only the vaguest notion of, or interest in, life past fifty. For them, the holy grail of advertising is the eighteen-to-forty-nine age group.

Ann A. Fishman, the president of the Generational-Targeted Marketing Corporation in New Orleans, recalls a meeting she once had at an ad agency in New York. "I was struck by the fact that every person I met except one was young," she said. "But you can't have one age group watching the store. You wind up not being sensitive to the various generational groups."

Gary Onks, an author and consultant who advises corporations on attracting older customers, also faults ad agencies and companies' advertising departments for being made up mainly of people twenty-five to thirty years old who "see only their own plateau." Younger people also forget about the elderly, in part, he said, "because of the increased divorced rates in recent decades and the breakdown of the traditional family, not to mention the mobility of Americans; as a result, a lot of younger people have lost contact with their grandparents and don't know how to bond with older people." He says this myopia about older people will change as seniors become a force that companies cannot ignore without the risk of declining sales. Smart companies, he contends, already recognize this. He often cites Borders bookstores and Cracker Barrel restaurants as examples of senior-friendly companies.

Borders, Onks writes in his book *Sold on Seniors: How You Can Reach and Sell the $20 Trillion Senior Marketplace* (Sold on Seniors Inc., 2001), makes it "so very easy to show up, browse, linger, and socialize: lots of chairs, sofas, helpers, refreshments, room to move about and excellent lighting." He adds: "Their stores simulate warm, cozy dens or family rooms. Seniors love it." Of Cracker Barrel restaurants, he writes: "These places literally ooze every aspect of marketing to seniors. The buildings themselves are designed to look like old country stores. The wide front porches are filled with rocking chairs, just like the front porches homes and stores used to have. The food is down-home, country-style cooking."

But a big problem for companies is that they might not attract aging boomers simply by shifting their products and ads toward an older audience. Remember, the boomers don't think of themselves as old. And they're not the only ones. A lot of current retirees in their sixties and seventies don't either.

Sam Craig, professor of marketing at New York University's Stern School of Business, agrees that there are a lot of untapped opportunities for the senior market. But he contends that mass-market advertisers sometimes appear to ignore seniors not out of ignorance but because of a "basic and subtle dilemma" rooted in the fact that a lot of older people, especially the baby boomers, have a youthful self-image. They don't want to be seen as old. "So if advertisers target the eighteen-to-forty-nine group, they will pick up some older viewers," Craig said. "But if they skew their ads to older viewers, they'll lose the younger ones as well as the older ones who don't see themselves as old. Companies are aware of the demographics, but if they target old they run the risk of being rejected by both groups." He added: "Look at ads specifically directed to older people, like those for vitamins. They don't

put people in these ads who are old and decrepit. They pick people who look younger, with gray hair the only real sign of aging.
They could be thirty-five year olds with prematurely gray hair."

New York ad executives Marian Salzman and Ira Matathia,
coauthors of *Next: Trends for the Near Future* (Overlook Press,
2000), wrote in a 2000 report to their clients: "From health care to
fashion, businesses will strive to keep up with a graying world. Yet
even as the trend continues, those at its center will be doing their
best to ignore it: Boomers have already succeeded in renaming
their middle age 'middle youth' and are using every tool at their
disposal to stave off the inevitable. Smart marketers will play along
with this mass delusion." Salzman put it more directly in an interview for my "Seniority" column in the *New York Times*: "The mass
delusion of the boomers is that you're never going to grow old,
that you will always look as good as you used to look," she said.
"You can sell boomers anything if they feel it's going to make them
sexy or more desirable."

But what about the dark side of delusion? What will happen to
the boomers when they really get old? Will they accept old age as
gracefully, say, as the GI generation that survived the Depression
and fought World War II? Or will there be an emotional and psychological collision at the junction of Delusion and Reality? Salzman thinks such a collision is a long-term possibility. "But right
now delusion is more powerful than the reality," she said. "What
we're going to see is people fighting back against the limitations of
age in ways we haven't seen before. The boomers will probably figure out a way to make adult diapers sexy."

Ken Dychtwald is troubled by the dark side of the boomer phe-
nomenon and our youth-obsessed culture; his concern is particularly reflected in one of his books, *Age Power: How the 21st
Century Will Be Ruled by the New Old* (J. P. Tarcher, 1999). The
book sees the aging of the population as a series of financial and
social disasters that can be prevented only through measures like
postponing the age at which people can collect Social Security

benefits and linking payments to the incomes of recipients—so-called means-testing. He also calls for limiting other entitlements, including Medicare, for older people.

Dychtwald said that while he liked to view the future optimistically, the study he did with Harris reinforced some of the negative possibilities he wrote about in *Age Power*. "While the study gives a lot of positive affirmations, I'm troubled by the high percentage of the population for whom old age is not a time of joy and pleasure and freedom, but a time of fear and pain and vulnerability," he said. "And remember, this is a generation that saved and had a lot of benefits—yet half of them are frightened and struggling in retirement. What does this mean for the baby boomers, who aren't going to have some of the benefits current retirees have? The Live for Todays and the Sick and Tireds might well multiply as boomers retire. Our youth-obsessed culture is concerned only with the here and now. We need to wake up to some of these long-term negative possibilities and as a society do more planning and preparing."

Boomers as a Resource

Theodore Roszak is decidedly not pessimistic about the huge numbers of retiring boomers and the graying of America. He, in fact, celebrates it. A history professor at the California State University at Hayward, he is the author of *Longevity Revolution: As Boomers Become Elders* (Berkeley Hills Books, 2001). In this paperback update of his 1998 book, *America the Wise*, he contends that the aging boomers will prove to be one of our culture's richest resources, not a burden. He argues forcefully and convincingly that the growing number of older people in America is a positive social development that should be nurtured, not a potential social and fiscal nightmare to be met with draconian measures. He sees opportunity where others see disaster in the Census Bureau projection that by 2020, people over sixty will make up 25 percent of the United States population.

Longevity Revolution views the boomers as a great asset, whose social value will increase as they grow older. This was a generation that in its youth was energetic and idealistic. He sees its members in their older years as compassionate and wise. In retirement, they will have the free time to return to their youthful impulses and devote themselves to good deeds. Instead of being a burden to their children, he maintains, the boomers will help support their children monetarily and provide other valuable services like child care.

Roszak is a staunch defender of entitlements for seniors. In *Longevity Revolution* he takes a swipe at the media, saying that it has accepted the language of Social Security critics and doomsayers ("demographic time bomb," "on the skids," "giant sponge soaking up so large a share of the federal budget"). He says journalists often have not checked data with the Social Security Administration, "whose veracity is unquestioned even by anti-entitlement critics." Using relatively modest growth projections, Roszak writes that the Social Security system will be solvent for at least thirty-plus years. He argues that if the Social Security payroll tax were to be raised by about 2 percentage points—half to be paid by employees, half by employers—the system would remain solvent through the rest of the century. That seems a modest proposal in a country whose citizens, as *Longevity Revolution* points out in a chapter on health care, spend three times as much on casino and lottery gambling as their government does on Medicare.

Roszak writes that the "crisis" in Social Security comes from two sources: powerful forces on Wall Street that want the business and stock trading commissions that would be generated from privatization of the system, and conservatives who have been hostile to the idea of government social insurance since it was created under the New Deal in 1935. The combination of those forces has proved fairly potent. Part of its success, Roszak argues, is the constant drumbeat of slanted statistics and misleading catchphrases from conservative policy institutes intended to cause panic over Social Security's future. How many times have you heard or read the phrase *looming insolvency* or something similar in discussions of Social Security?

Perhaps as many times as you've heard or read that you need 70 to 80 percent of your preretirement income to retire successfully.

One of the by-products of an aging population is a shrinking pool of younger workers, which can have profound consequences for corporate America. Many companies that once practiced subtle and not-so-subtle age discrimination may soon find themselves fiercely competing to retain older workers. Bill Zinke, a consultant for corporations on hiring and retraining older workers, wants to change the "national mind-set" about older Americans. "The general attitude is that when you reach a certain age, you're over the hill," he said. "You should go somewhere and enjoy the 'golden years.'" Zinke, a former corporate and criminal lawyer in New York, runs his own consulting company, Human Resource Services, in Boulder, Colorado. He is an example of what he preaches. He is seventy-six years old and has no plans to retire. "We should not see aging and our increased longevity in a negative light," he said, echoing Theodore Roszak. "Instead of worrying about the graying of America, we should be looking forward to the benefits and opportunities of this demographic change. An older population is also a wiser and more skilled population."

"The Dream Was Always There"

The next time a youth-obsessed advertising agency convenes a focus group to divine how to spend a client's money, maybe Jack McQuillan should be included. McQuillan, sixty-eight, has fulfilled a long-held dream that would tax the imagination, drive, and pocketbook of someone half his age. A retired New York City detective sergeant from Staten Island, McQuillan earned a private pilot's license—despite medical problems that might have turned someone less determined to shuffleboard. He has dreamed of that achievement since he was seven. As a boy, McQuillan hung around a small airport on Staten Island, sometimes scraping together $2 for an airplane ride. The airfield has long since been replaced by the Staten Island Mall, but that early love of flying stayed with him through a four-year stint in the marine corps and thirty-four years on the police force. "I was just always too busy working, and my money had to go for raising a family," he said. "But the dream was always there."

Finally, in 1990—nearing retirement and his four children on their own—McQuillan finally realized his dream and started taking flying lessons at a private flight school in New Jersey. The dream, however, almost ended. Because he is an insulin-dependent diabetic, he could not pass the physical examination required by the Federal Aviation Administration for a private pilot's license. He continued taking lessons for a couple of years because he loved flying so much, although he knew it would not lead to a pilot's license. "I was pretty discouraged," he recalled. He retired in 1996, at age sixty, still harboring dreams of flying.

Then, in 1997, the FAA changed the rules and allowed insulin-dependent diabetics to fly, with certain restrictions and more rigorous and more frequent medical exams. "I was back in the game," he beamed. Since starting lessons in 1990 and resuming them in 1997, he has had successful cataract surgery in both eyes, suffered a broken ankle, and undergone prostate surgery. In 2000, he and his wife moved from Staten Island to Millbrook, New York, in Dutchess County, where he switched to another flight school. His training there was interrupted for a time by restrictions in the aftermath of the September 11, 2001, terrorist attacks on the World Trade Center. But he persevered and was awarded his private pilot's license on August 23, 2002. He was sixty-six years old.

For McQuillan, retirement helped fulfill a dream that he had clung to across the decades. "You know how everybody has a dream in which they are flying?" he said. "Well, flying low and slow in a small plane is as close as you can come to that dream in this life." His advice for a successful retirement: "Keep going. Stay active. Don't vegetate."

2

What the Experts Say You Need versus What You Really Need

Remember, You Need 80% of Your Income to Retire!
— SIGN IN A NEW JERSEY BANK

Congratulations! You've made the decision that retirement is for you. You are ready to enter the next phase of your life and pursue other interests and goals. But can you afford it? Unless you're sixty-two, you can't collect Social Security benefits. Do you have enough savings to produce an income stream you can realistically live on? And even if you are sixty-two and eligible for reduced Social Security benefits, there are limits on how much you can earn from working until you are sixty-five (see chapter 7). That can be important because you may actually want to work, perhaps on a part-time or freelance basis, at something you've always been interested in but never had time for.

PROJECTIONS: REALISTIC AND OTHERWISE

As we work through these questions, the most important thing to remember is to question and be skeptical of most of the so-called experts, especially those who quote data from the mutual fund and equities industries showing that you need at least 70 percent, and preferably 80 percent, of your preretirement income in order to retire. These estimates of retirement needs are self-serving, generated by companies that have a vested interest in convincing people to save as much as possible—with the mutual funds or brokerage firms, of course.

Charles Schwab, head of the big discount brokerage firm that bears his name, writes in his book *You're Fifty—Now What?: Investing for the Second Half of Your Life* (Crown, 2000) that while the minimum percentage of your income you will need to retire is 70 percent, he is much more comfortable with 80 percent. He even tries to make the case that sometimes a retired person may need 100 percent—or more!

There have been many magazine and newspaper articles pointing out that Americans are retiring later, reversing a decades-long trend toward early retirements. These articles are based on surveys, mainly of baby boomers, that show that boomers plan to continue working past the traditional retirement age of sixty-five. Many of those surveyed cited their meager savings and cutbacks in company pensions and medical coverage as factors that have led them to believe that they can't opt out early. But these articles ignore a very important reason that many people think they have to work longer: the constant drumbeat from the mutual fund and equities industries—and financial writers, planners, and advisers who rely on their data—that without 70 to 80 percent of their preretirement income, retirees will end up impoverished.

All these inflated projections assume, of course, that you make no changes in your lifestyle or level of expenses when you retire. Well, before you make any commitments to work longer or resign yourself to a bread line, take a deep breath and consider the advice of Fred E. Waddell.

Waddell, a semiretired money-management specialist in Smith

Mountain Lake, Virginia, trains financial counselors. He contends that estimates of how much you need to retire are unrealistically inflated by the mutual fund and equities industries and accuses them of "fear selling" to attract customers and their money. "The mutual fund industry persists in using these inflated figures because they have a vested interest in doing so," said Waddell, who is a retired associate professor from Auburn University in Alabama. "This frightens people into thinking they're going to need a great deal more in savings than they really will. As a result, people over-save for retirement or put off retiring. These unrealistic projections can also be psychologically depressing for a lot of people who think they'll never have quite enough."

The projections are flawed, according to Waddell, because they are based on *preretirement income* rather than on *postretirement expenses*. "Most older people, with their children gone and expenses down, are saving as much as they can in anticipation of retirement," he said. "They may be living on forty percent or less of their disposable income and saving the rest. In my case, I was living on thirty-five to forty percent of my take-home pay, and I think I was typical. Well, when you retire you don't have to save for retirement anymore. So right now I'm living on a hundred percent of my preretirement disposable income, which was only thirty-five to forty percent of my total salary." He continued: "When people say you need X percent of preretirement income, it defies explanation. It's a huge mistake to base these projections on income rather than expenses. The only sensible way is to compare your expenses, preretirement and postretirement. For financial planners to ignore these common-sense considerations raises questions about their objectivity."

Another example of the mutual fund industry's hype that Waddell likes to point out is its tendency to overestimate the future rate of inflation to convince clients that they need to save even more to retire. Estimating future inflation at 4 percent a year rather than a more realistic 3 percent may not sound like a big deal. But remember, the difference between 4 percent and 3 percent is not 1 percent, but 1 *percentage point*. The real difference is 33.3 percent, which means the growth of your future retirement expense are being overstated by one-third!

Waddell says that some financial counselors who work for big firms have telephoned him and, while refusing to give their names, have told him he is exactly right on this issue. "They will tell me they can't give their names because they would get in trouble with their firms, where the policies are to rake in as much money as possible with the line that you need seventy to eighty percent of preretirement income to retire," he said.*

Not every expense, however, will decrease when you retire. Waddell points out that if you are not sixty-five, and thus ineligible for Medicare—and your company's retirement plan has no health insurance benefit—your medical expenses may increase, especially if you have to buy health insurance. According to government figures, he said, the average increase for pre-Medicare medical expense for retirees is 125 percent. "A lot of retirees want to travel, so expenses related to that may also increase, but usually only temporarily," he added.

Waddell's advice is wise. But he and others like him are drowned out by the advertising and public relations powers of big mutual funds and brokers. The result is that many Americans have bought into Wall Street's slick sell as they approach the final decade or so of their working lives. Those who started saving late, like many of the estimated 70 million baby boomers who are famous for spending instead of saving, often are convinced that they can't afford early retirement and will have to work much longer than they

*In the almost six years that I have been writing the "Seniority" column for the *New York Times*, I have from time to time discussed the notion that people don't need as much to retire as they have been told by stockbrokers and mutual fund salesmen. Whenever I have written about this, I have received scores of letters and e-mail messages from readers agreeing with me and thanking me for pointing it out. I have yet to receive a single letter or message from anyone in the financial services industry arguing otherwise.

would like. Some, in a panic, have become born-again savers in an effort to play catch-up, pouring billions of dollars into the mutual funds and stocks that helped fuel the bull market of the 1990s. They watch every twitch of the Dow. Their angst is palpable. When the market slumps, they joke about having to work until they are eighty.

Mind you, I am not opposed to saving. More is usually better than less. What I am opposed to is continuing to work when what you really want to do is retire or perhaps change course. This is especially true if you are burned out or in a dead-end job, as many people in their middle to late fifties find themselves. I believe that most people can retire from wage slavery sooner than they think if they are willing to pay a relatively painless price for their freedom: a simpler, downsized life and, perhaps, a move to a less expensive part of the country—and it doesn't have to be remote or far away. This is especially true for those living in expensive, high-tax urban centers on both coasts.

So relax. It can be done, especially if you are willing to make that move to a cheaper location and learn to live within or *slightly beneath* your means. I first began to realize that the mutual fund data was out of kilter when I would travel from the New York City area to visit friends and relatives in the Midwest and South. I was struck by how well they were living on relatively small incomes, at least compared with New York and California. But hold on, you say, I don't want to move to another part of the country. That's okay. You can still retire on less than you think, especially if you are willing to make a short-distance move. More about this and a simpler life—emphasizing your capacity to focus on the few things that are really important to your freedom and happiness—later. First, the two most important keys to being able to retire on less than you think are your house, which is most people's biggest single asset, and your health insurance.

You need enough equity in your current home to be able to pay cash for a new home in whatever area of the country you choose for retirement; if you elect to stay put, and you are at least sixty-two years old, you may need the equity for a reverse mortgage to boost your income. (Chapter 5 looks at reverse mortgages and the housing issue in depth.)

Because Medicare isn't available until you are sixty-five, you must have health insurance. Don't even think of trying to live without it. One serious illness could put you on the welfare rolls. Only about 30 percent of employers offer any retirement health benefits, so you may have to buy this insurance on your own. Chapter 6 looks at various alternatives available to make sure you're covered until you reach the eligibility age for Medicare.

For working through the numbers at this point, we're going to make the assumptions that you have the necessary home equity and that you are willing to make that move to a cheaper region. The final part of this chapter will deal with those who want to remain in the area where they have always lived.

CRUNCHING SOME NUMBERS

Let's take a hypothetical case and look at the figures.

Joe and Sue Sample are both fifty-nine. They own their own home in an affluent suburb of New York. They have two sons who are grown and living independently. Joe commutes to Manhattan where he is an editor for a chain of medical newsletters; Sue is a teacher at a private school in the town where they live. Their combined income is $150,000 a year. Like many baby boomers, they got serious about saving only twelve years ago, when they began putting the maximum into their company 401(k) plans. However, they invested mostly in stock funds, and the market boom of the 1990s has given them a 401(k) nest egg of $300,000, most of which they luckily switched into bond and money-market funds in 2001 when stocks began a clear slide from their highs. They also have a rainy-day fund of $30,000 in bank certificates of deposit.

Joe and Sue would like to retire in six months when they are both sixty, even though they can't collect Social Security until they are sixty-two—and then at a reduced rate. Their Social Security may also be reduced a bit further because, if they retire at sixty, their income will drop during the two years between retirement and age sixty-two. This will somewhat affect the calculation that determines the amount of their monthly Social Security benefits (more on this in chapter 7).

They would like to move to a less congested and warmer area where they can indulge year-round their passion for bicycling. But they don't think they have nearly enough money. They have read that they need 70 to 80 percent of their current income—or $105,000 to $120,000—to retire. Sue has no pension at her job to supplement the savings in her 401(k) plan. Joe has changed jobs several times over the years and has been at his current position for only fourteen years. He will be eligible for a pension plan—in addition to his 401(k) plan—when he is sixty, but will receive only $1,500 a month, or $18,000 a year; if he waits until he is sixty-six (for the couple's age group, the full Social Security retirement age has been raised to sixty-six from sixty-five), his pension will be $1,800 a month, or $21,600 a year. In addition, he will get $200 a month, or $2,400 a year, from a previous employer's pension plan, in which he barely vested. At age sixty, these two income sources will total $1,700 a month, or $20,400 a year. Most financial advisers would probably agree that Joe and Sue could safely take 4 percent a year, or $12,000, from their $300,000 nest egg without fear of using it up while they are still living. This would boost their annual income to $32,400—only a fraction of the $105,000 minimum. Using the nest egg to further increase their income to the $105,000 level would devour the $300,000 in short order.

If they wait until they are sixty-two and can begin collecting combined, and reduced, Social Security benefits of about $2,200 a month, or $26,400 a year, they would have a total income of $58,800—still only slightly more than half of the minimum they have been told they must have. The Samples are worried that they may have to work until they are sixty-six and eligible for full Social Security benefits, which will give them a combined pay-out of about $3,100 a month, or $37,200 a year. That would lift their total annual income to $75,200, boosted a bit by Joe's big-ger pension, which jumps to $1,800 when he hits sixty-six, and by the assumption that their nest egg has grown to $350,000; 4 percent of that gives them $14,000 a year. But the $75,200 is still well shy of the $105,000 mark—which by the way has now grown to almost $118,000, assuming the couple's annual com-bined income rose 3 percent a year to $168,000.

Now they are afraid they may have to work until they are sev-enty and delay collecting Social Security until then, when their combined monthly government benefit will have risen to $4,300, or $51,600 a year. Figure 1 shows their income and its sources at various retirement ages.

However, even if Joe and Sue wait until they are seventy, they will still fall short of the mutual fund industry's projection of 70 percent, or $105,000, which actually will have grown to $140,000 assuming their combined salary increases 3 percent a year for ten years, to just under $200,000. The $51,600 from Social Security plus the $24,000 from Joe's two pensions—the first, smaller one was capped when he left the job to which it was linked; the second is capped when he reaches sixty-six—total $75,600. Let's assume, conservatively, that their nest egg has grown to $400,000 by the time they're seventy. The 4 percent annually they can take from that comes to $16,000. That still gives them only $91,600 a year—a $13,400 shortfall, compared with the lower $105,000 projection, and a whopping $48,400 gap when compared with the $140,000 projection based on the reasonable expectation of 3 percent annual salary increases. It gets even worse if you use the 80 percent benchmark instead of

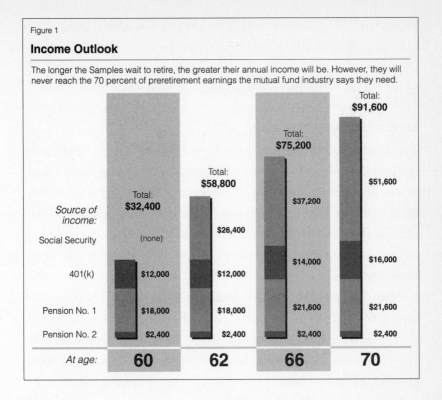

Figure 1

Income Outlook

The longer the Samples wait to retire, the greater their annual income will be. However, they will never reach the 70 percent of preretirement earnings the mutual fund industry says they need.

Source of income:	At age: 60	At age: 62	At age: 66	At age: 70
	Total: $32,400	Total: $58,800	Total: $75,200	Total: $91,600
Social Security	(none)	$26,400	$37,200	$51,600
401(k)	$12,000	$12,000	$14,000	$16,000
Pension No. 1	$18,000	$18,000	$21,600	$21,600
Pension No. 2	$2,400	$2,400	$2,400	$2,400

70 percent. Just imagine if Joe and Sue bound themselves to Charles Schwab's estimate of 100 percent! They wonder if they will ever be able to retire.

Let's take a closer look at their situation and apply some more realistic projections and estimates to their problem. I have tried to use figures that are as accurate and current as possible. The Social Security benefit estimates, for instance, are based on Social Security Administration data. As a reality check, I found friends whose incomes matched the Samples' and borrowed their Social Security projections—the ones included in periodic mailings from the SSA that tell what you can roughly expect to receive at your full retirement age, as well as sixty-two and seventy. Where I have been forced to make estimates, I have usually based them on my own experiences or the experiences of relatives and friends. Also, while some of the numbers—especially prices—will probably have changed by the time this book is published, the relative differences will likely be very similar. On balance, I think what follows is reasonably accurate.

Location, Location, Location

There are two free Web sites, www.BestPlaces.net and www. RetirementLiving.com, that help expose the exaggerated estimates of retirement needs by the mutual fund and stock industries. The sites allow you to compare the cost of living among cities around the country, using data from excellent sources, including federal and state governments. (RetirementLiving.com deals more specifically with taxes in the various states. Both these sites will be discussed in greater detail in chapter 4.) BestPlaces.net shows, for instance, that if you make $100,000 a year in New York City, you need to make only $41,134 a year—or 41 percent of your New York salary—to maintain a *comparable* lifestyle in Jacksonville, Florida. If Tucson, Arizona, is more to your liking, you'll need $42,327, or 42 percent. Remember, *these comparisons assume you make no changes in your lifestyle*, that you continue to pay a mortgage and maintain the same standard of living, including work expenses like commuting, clothes, and lunches. Imagine how much lower these income requirements would be if we eliminated mortgage payments and work expenses. The numbers can go lower still if you trim other spending to achieve a less expensive lifestyle.

Why do members of the mutual fund industry tell you that if you make $100,000, you'll need $70,000 to $80,000 to retire? They want your money. It's that simple.

It's the Expenses, Stupid

Let's apply some of the data from the BestPlaces.net and RetirementLiving.com Web sites and from other sources to Joe and

Sue's situation, keeping in mind Fred Waddell's advice to focus on expenses, not income. In addition, let's assume that Joe and Sue would be happy to retire to Tucson, where the climate suits their love of bicycling.

The couple's house is a four-bedroom Dutch colonial. They bought it ten years ago for $185,000 and spent another $20,000 on repairs and upgrades, including installing a new heating system and rewiring the entire house. They owe $140,000 on their mortgage. Their monthly house payment is $1,000; their property tax is $715 a month, or $8,580 a year, a figure not uncommon in the New York area. There has been a rapid rise in real estate values in their town, which is within easy commuting distance of midtown Manhattan; if they sold their house today it would likely fetch $350,000. After a 6 percent, or $21,000, real estate agent's fee, they could walk away from their house with $189,000. Under current law, that money is tax-free.

The Samples owe $15,000 on a car they bought new last year. Their car payment is $375 a month. They have a second car, which is ten years old and long since paid for. They have another $20,000 of debt in a bank overdraft and various credit card bills. These payments total $500 a month.

The couple's utilities run about $250 a month. In addition, they pay about $170 a month for life insurance and $160 a month for auto insurance—they live in one of the most expensive areas of the nation for car insurance. Their homeowner's insurance, $650 a year, is included in the mortgage payment. Joe's commuting expenses come to $220 a month, and he spends another $150 a month for lunches in Manhattan. Sue takes her lunch to school. Together, Joe and Sue estimate they spend $3,600 a year on clothes that they need for their jobs. Their health insurance, provided by Joe's employer, is through an HMO, so they have few out-of-pocket medical expenses.

They spend about $800 a month for food and dining out.

Let's examine these core expenses on a monthly and yearly basis:

	Monthly	Yearly
Mortgage	$1,000	$12,000
Property tax	$715	$8,580
Car payment	$375	$4,500
Credit cards, etc.	$500	$6,000
Utilities	$250	$3,000
Insurance (all)	$330	$3,960
Commuting/lunches	$370	$4,440
Clothes	$300	$3,600
Food/dining out	$800	$9,600
Totals	$4,640	$55,680

Now clearly the Samples have more expenses than those listed above. There are bills for vacations, car maintenance, and home repairs, to name a few. I have not included taxes, other than property taxes, in the calculations so far. But let's use this snapshot of their core, nonvariable expenses in considering their retirement needs.

Imagine they decide to retire to Tucson, where it is almost 58 percent less expensive to live than in New York, according to BestPlaces.net. First they sell their house and pocket the $189,000. They spend $35,000 of that to pay off their car, credit card bills, and bank overdraft. That leaves them with $154,000. They use $4,000 of that to move to Arizona, leaving them with $150,000.

According to BestPlaces.net, housing costs—including taxes and related expenses—in Tucson are slightly below the national average. New York City, partly because expensive Manhattan apartment rents are included in the calculations, is more than four times the national average. The New York suburbs, depending on location, can be two to three times the national average. The median price—meaning half are above and half below—of a home in Tucson is $120,240. This compares with about $275,000 in the Samples' suburban New York town and $146,102 nationwide.

Do you see where this is leading?

The Samples can take the $150,000 left from the sale of their house and pay cash for, say, a $120,000 home in Tucson and have $30,000 left to add to the $30,000 they already have in the bank for a rainy day. Suddenly their mortgage payment disappears. Their property taxes drop from $8,580 a year, or $715 a month, to $1,320 a year, or $110 a month.

Gone are commuting and other work-related expenses. The Arizona state income tax works out to 3.9 percent, or $1,950, on a $50,000 income; the national average is 4.6 percent on a $50,000 income. In New York, the Samples were paying more than $6,000 in state taxes. In addition, Arizona is one of twenty-six states that does not tax Social Security benefits (see chapter 4).

In Tucson, the couple's food bills will drop by almost one-third. They will need only one car, and their auto insurance—which is much less expensive in Arizona than in the New York area—will drop to $870 a year, or $72.50 a month, from $1,920 a year, or $160 a month.

Suddenly, the $32,400 a year, or $2,700 a month, they will have if they retire at age sixty looks a whole lot better, especially when you realize that they will have no mortgage or rent to pay.

In fact, let's look at what's left of the Samples' estimated core expenses after the hypothetical move to Arizona. The amounts are based on data from various sources, including BestPlaces.net and RetirementLiving.com. The figures for clothing are based on my own estimate using some general cost-of-living data and personal experience. The same goes for food and dining out.

	Monthly	Yearly
Mortgage	$0	$0
Property taxes	$110	$1,320
Car payment	$0	$0
Credit cards, etc.	$0	$0
Utilities	$200	$2,400
Insurance (all)	$338	$4,056
Commuting/lunches	$0	$0
Clothes	$100	$1,200
Food/dining out	$600	$7,200
Totals	$1,348	$16,176

The increased insurance costs represent life insurance premiums of $170 a month, a constant; auto insurance premiums of $72.50 (rounded to $73); $45 a month for homeowner's insurance, which had previously been included in the mortgage payment; and the addition of $50 a month that Joe must pay for company-provided retiree health benefits, which also cover Sue.

Joe and Sue are lucky. His company provides retirees, even those like him who take early retirement after only fifteen years of service, with the same health insurance they had when they were working for the nominal fee of only $50 a month. Still, even if they had been forced to buy health insurance, it would not have broken their budget (see chapter 6).

Remember, the Samples only have to live on their current retirement income of $2,700 a month, or $32,400 a year, for two years. At sixty-two, they can start collecting Social Security benefits of $2,200 a month, or $26,400 a year—bringing their total income then to $58,800. If they find they need more cash during these first two years of retirement, they could cash in one or both of their life insurance policies, which may no longer be such a high priority (see chapter 3). Of course, they could tap into their rainy-day fund, which is now $60,000.

The Samples could also take part-time jobs for a couple of years until Social Security kicks in. But when they start to collect Social Security at sixty-two, Joe and Sue will face limitations on how much they can earn without reducing their benefits; at full retirement age, those limitations vanish (see chapter 7).

Joe and Sue should be able to live, and pedal, well within their means in Tucson without having to turn to any of these extra measures.

Portfolios Still Count

Deena Katz, the financial adviser mentioned in chapter 1, agreed that 4 percent was a reasonable amount that the Samples could withdraw each year from their 401(k) plan. But she warned that the $300,000 in their portfolio should be split among several investment choices, including stocks, so that over time their savings are not eaten away by inflation. And she stressed the importance of taking inflation into account when considering returns. "How you take out your money is as important as how you accumulate it," she said. "When people retire, they intuitively want to put all their money into fixed-income investments. That's a mistake. It won't keep up with inflation. Say your money's in a fixed-income fund earning six percent. You take out four percent a year. Inflation is three percent. That means you're losing one percent a year."

That could mean seriously eroded savings when you're older and your need for the money may be more critical.

In the case of Joe and Sue Sample, Katz recommended that they segment their $300,000 portfolio in the following manner:

- 60 percent, or $180,000, in stocks, which have the potential to appreciate in value over time. "Historical data say that sixty percent is likely to allow the portfolio to last the rest of their lives, assuming they keep the modest four percent drawdown amount," she said. However, she added that in the wake of the

1990s boom, she expected to see very low returns in the next
decade or so.
- $24,000 in a money market fund. This is the amount that the
Samples want to withdraw over the next two years.
- The remaining $96,000 divided in bond funds with bonds of various maturities of up to ten years.

"Then every year or so," Katz continued, "they should rebalance the portfolio along these lines, using proceeds—when possible—to replenish the money market fund for their two years' worth of withdrawals. Some years there may not be enough proceeds, and they may have to dip into the principal in the bond funds. But other years there will be more than enough from the proceeds and they won't have to touch the principal; the extra proceeds will become part of the principal, keeping their portfolio strong. This way they don't need to sell stock to get money to live on and thus are never forced to sell stock in a down market. The only time they may need to sell stock is when it's gone up."

The Moving Story

Bert Sperling is the chief executive of Fast Forward, the Portland, Oregon, company that runs www.BestPlaces.net. The site contains figures for 330 metropolitan areas, where Sperling says 75 percent of the population lives. The site also includes data on most cities and towns with populations of 10,000 or more. The company makes money by selling data to corporations and publications like *Money* magazine that publish "Best Places" articles on where to live or retire. "If people are willing to change their place of living and change their pace of life," Sperling said, "then there are significant savings to be had."

Sperling concedes, however, that many people may not want to retire to less urban areas or be far from their families or where they have spent most of their lives. "We're used to cities, and for some people that's going to be tough to give up," he said. "But the best of both worlds is to move to a small town within an hour or so of one of these metro areas. You have inexpensive small-town living but are still within easy driving distance of the benefits of health care, arts, and culture that cities offer."

www.RetirementLiving.com. is operated by the Retirement Living Information Center in Redding, Connecticut. It has several categories on retirement living, but the section on state taxes is one of the most useful and popular. The state tax section lays out the facts on each state, but cites no favorites. "We don't make recommendations because of people's different lifestyles and needs," said Tom Wetzel, president of the Retirement Living Information Center. Visitors to the Web site can sign up for a free monthly newsletter via e-mail. Chapter 4 takes a close look at living costs and taxes in various states and regions.

Both Web site operators stress the value of planning. "Retirement is very important," Sperling said. "It's worth a little bit of research and fact-finding."

Now let's assume that Joe and Sue Sample want to retire, but don't want to move far from the New York area.

The key to making this work remains the sale of their house and paying off their outstanding bills, just as they did in the hypothetical move to Arizona. In this scenario, they take Sperling's advice and find a smaller, less expensive house, perhaps farther away from New York City but still in the general region. Western New Jersey and eastern Pennsylvania, for example, offer much less expensive places to live that are within a drive of an hour or so from Manhattan. In fact, the figures for Allentown, Pennsylvania, which is less than a two-hour drive from New York, are comparable to those for Tucson (home prices, in fact, are less). The same is true for Bethlehem, Pennsylvania, which is actually a bit closer to New York than Allentown. Pennsylvania's tax structure is also favorable to retirees.

The closer you get to New York, the higher the numbers go. This could mean that the Samples might have to use some of the $30,000 from the sale of their house that they were able to put in the bank when they moved to Tucson to instead help produce income for a couple of years until they can collect Social Security. Or, they may have to trim their discretionary spending a bit more here and there.

What if the Samples insist on retiring right where they are, in their same house and neighborhood? Well, the hard truth is, they may not be able to do it—not with their big house payment and property tax bill. It could be doable if we change their hypothetical situation and, for instance, assume their home is fully paid for and that they are sixty-two and eligible for Social Security benefits and a reverse mortgage, which could be used to pay property taxes. In their present circumstances, they are probably going to have to relocate. That could mean selling their house and moving to a smaller, less expensive home in the same area—if they can find one. They might have to move to one of those smaller towns with relatively easy access to the more expensive New York area.

But would that be so bad?

I know that most surveys by AARP and others show that the majority of those questioned say they want to retire right where they are. I wonder if those surveyed would answer the same way if the question explained that in order to do that they might have to delay their retirement by three, five, seven, or ten years and have much less discretionary income than if they moved to a less expensive place? Is having to drive an hour or two to visit family and old friends so difficult? Might it be worth it if you could retire earlier and in greater financial comfort? And if you're moving to another area of the country, you're never more than a few hours away by plane; you can always pick a spot with easy access to a major airport hub, which usually means cheaper flights.

Moving to a new place can be an adventure, a chance to meet new friends and have new experiences. Don't reject it out of hand.

Whatever you do, the most important element is having a home that is paid for or has enough equity, as in the case of the Samples, to allow you to sell it and buy another, less expensive home free and clear or to tap into your current home's equity through a reverse mortgage if you are sixty-two. This is the key that unlocks the possibility of retiring early for most people.

Your personal situation may be similar to that of Joe and Sue Sample, or it may be very different. Chapter 8 contains worksheets so that you can figure out your own road to retiring early on less than you think.

It can be done. And the reward for doing it is freedom.

SOME IMPORTANT LESSONS

If you're still doubtful, let's take a look at two real-life examples of people who have successfully retired on much less than the experts said they could and have refocused their lives in ways that are more meaningful to them. While you may not want to live exactly as they do, their experiences can teach us some important lessons.

"The Happiest Guy in Texas"

I call Elton Pasea a mutual fund salesman's worst nightmare. I interviewed Pasea, who is eighty-one and a native of Trinidad, in 1998 for my first "Seniority" column in the *New York Times*. At that time, he was living quite nicely in Nederland, Texas, on $1,200 a month: $700 from Social Security and $500 from a union pension.

Very little has changed in his circumstances since then. His monthly Social Security check has increased to $812, raising his total income to $1,312 a month, or $15,744 a year. "I'm loaded now," he said. "I'm having the time of my life." He owns his own home and has about $47,000—his life's savings—invested in bank certificates of deposit. He has never owned stocks, bonds, or mutual funds. "I don't know anything about stocks," said Pasea, a widower. "I've never even considered them."

He apparently has never considered that, according to projections by mutual fund companies, he should be eating cat food—or at least wallowing in financial misery, sorry that he didn't take the companies' advice and save more. He doesn't have a million-dollar nest egg, and his income isn't at least 70 percent of his preretirement figure that the projections say he needs. How can the poor wretch possibly be having a good time? The reality is that the Elton Paseas of this world are living proof that many such estimates of retirement needs are self-serving, designed to entice people to pour money into mutual funds and stocks.

Pasea retired to Nederland on the Gulf Coast in 1984 after forty-one years of roaming the world as a merchant seaman. He wanted a small town and a warm climate in which to indulge his lifelong passion: bicycling. He rides every day and racks up about four thousand miles a year. He takes a couple of big bicycle trips a year—one of them usually in Europe—all within his annual income of $15,744. On his overseas bicycle trips he often saves money by staying in youth hostels.

He doesn't have many health-related expenses. Wiry and fit from all that riding, he also watches his diet, which consists mostly of fish and vegetables, and he has never smoked.

Pasea's modest house is paid for. If it needs repairs, he usually does them himself. Texas has no state income tax, and his property taxes run a little less than $400 a year. His utility bills average $100 a month. He drives a 1984 Nissan with "only" 246,000 miles on the odometer, so at some point he may have to dip into his savings to replace it.

In 1998, he was often living on less than $500 a month and using the rest for travel or savings. Now, he says, at eighty-one he is less concerned about saving. "But it's difficult for me to spend thirteen hundred dollars a month," he said. "It takes very little for me to live." However, he does not stint when it comes to bicycles.

He has spent about $3,000 on his two high-performance road bikes and related equipment. Music is another passion. An amateur musician who used to play the clarinet, Pasea sometimes splurges on CDs—modern classical (his "first love") and jazz. And the reward of such a Spartan life? "I'm the happiest guy in Texas," Pasea said.

"A Meaningful Life"

In 1987, at the age of fifty-five, James McCain retired early from a teaching career at a university where he was an associate professor of American studies. He did so in order to have the time to complete a book on the history of ranching in the Southwest that he had begun four years earlier.

In 1990 he and his wife moved to a small town in New Mexico, where she had been hired as a public health nurse. He continued his research and writing and they subsequently bought a modest bungalow on six acres close to a national forest area. This gave them the space they needed to keep horses they both loved.

They paid $50,000 down from the sale of their former house on the new $65,000 property and took out a mortgage for the remaining $15,000. With McCain's reduced retirement income of less than $1,000 a month, along with his wife's nursing salary, the two lived quite comfortably.

The ranching book was published in 1993. It was his third book. While teaching at the university, he had published another history and a biography. The ranching book, never intended as a best seller, received superior reviews from academic historians.

But the next year McCain and his wife divorced. In the settlement, she took all the couple's savings—$30,000—and he got the house and the mortgage. Suddenly McCain was faced with having to maintain himself, the house, and a substantial piece of property with considerably less money than he had anticipated. As he put it, "Our investment here was a two-income proposition, and now I was stuck with the investment and one income." But he had a keen sense of what he wanted: freedom and the independence to live and work on his on terms, and he was willing to make sacrifices for that kind of life.

His response should be instructive to all those who think they can't afford to retire. "I could have gone back to work or taken a part-time job at Wal-Mart or McDonald's," he said. "I did work part-time for a while. But working for someone else was truly a waste of my time." Instead, he organized his life and finances in such a way that he is able to live within his modest income, although he concedes that he usually "lives along the edge." He calls himself an "edgemaster." Nevertheless, his life is not without cultural comforts. He drives to El Paso for classical concerts and is active in the literary life of the Southwest.

He has no expectations of making money from his books. "When I quit teaching to finish the ranching book, it was not primarily a financial decision," he said. "My research for the ranch history was all archival work, and it took a lot of travel to get to the sources. I couldn't do it while teaching full-time. Survival was important, sure, but money wasn't."

His lifestyle is not for everyone. For instance, he continued to keep two horses while driving, until recently, a 1977 Volkswagen Beetle with a twice-rebuilt engine and 400,000 on the odometer. He also owns a 1959 Chevrolet pickup, which he bought for $450 in 1974. He uses it to pull his horse trailer and to haul wood for his stove and feed for the horses.

Most of his monthly income is from two sources: his university pension, now $1,043, and a Social Security check for about $860. This gives him an annual income of $22,836. In addition, he usually makes a few hundred dollars a year from book royalties and other writing.

Like Elton Pasea, McCain owns no stocks or bonds. He used to have a small stock portfolio, but its value declined dramatically in the market crash of 1987. He then got out of stocks altogether, realizing that he didn't have the temperament for the market's ups and downs nor the interest in learning how to manage stock investments. His father and his grandfather, both economic victims of the Great Depression, had taught him that stock investments were risky.

Until recently, he had $7,000 in a savings account at a local bank. But he used almost $5,000 of that to buy a 1995 Volkswagen Golf to replace his vintage Beetle, which he sold for $2,455. In 1999, he used his savings to pay off the $9,000 that remained on his home mortgage. He later took out a reverse mortgage on his home and six acres to buy an adjoining six acres, giving him a total of twelve acres. He estimates the value of his house and expanded property at about $225,000, though the debt for the additional six acres is now approximately $65,000.

His core monthly expenses are minimal: $125 for utilities; $165 for a Medigap health insurance policy; $250 for food; $100 for homeowner and auto insurance; $42 for property taxes; and $150 to maintain and feed his two horses. Because he is a Korean War veteran and his income is below a certain level, he is able to get prescription medicines through the Veterans Administration for a small co-pay. "But I have to spend a good bit to maintain this place and my car and truck," he said. "I have to be prepared for things breaking down. For instance, I recently had to buy a $400 pressure tank for my well and had to reshingle my house. I cut corners everywhere I can. I usually car camp when I travel, which is easy to do in the West. I rarely eat out. If I want to buy something I have to save the money for it. I can't afford payments and interest. But I'm unable to save on a regular basis; at the end of the month if I can stick $100 in savings, I do. I've made sacrifices in order to have the freedom to focus on the very few things I most like, the things that give me a really meaningful life."

McCain, now seventy-two, has recently published a revised paperback edition of his ranch history, as well as another book, an account of Santa Fe before the Civil War. He is currently at work on a military history of Kansas. His books are truly a labor of love. Although highly regarded, none has ever recovered even the expense of the research and writing. "I write things that need to be written," he said, "not things in order to sell. It might be nice to sell loads of books, but that's not my real purpose. I have a low income compared with others in my age group with my education and experience. I have given up things that most people wouldn't think of giving up, like expensive trips, fancy cars, and RVs. But I manage to live pretty well. I'm blessed in being able to live the life of a rich man without a rich man's income." He figures that in a pinch, he could sell lots off his twelve acres as home sites. But he calls that a last resort. He doesn't want to risk noisy neighbors. Sitting on his porch in the late evening, under the clear, star-filled New Mexico sky and looking at the mountains, it's easy to understand why.

Despite his limited income, McCain says he has thrived in "retirement" because he has an "old-time attitude." "I grew up in the Great Depression," he said. "My philosophy is to 'make do.' I drive an old car and truck, and I repair things instead of buying new. You've got to be willing to darn your own socks and shoe your own horses. That's a reality for me, but it's also a metaphor for the price of my freedom. That's the way I've chosen to live in order to have the freedom I desire. And, by the way, I take pride in being able to shoe my horses. Not many men at my age still do that. But to do what I do you probably have to live in a part of the country where property prices and taxes are lower. It'd be impossible to live as well as I do—to live on twelve acres with two horses, not to mention a whole national forest and two great wilderness areas out my back door—on my income in northern New Jersey, for example."

What this all really boils down to, he repeats, is living a meaningful life as you define it. "There are two ways to live at my age," he said. "You can have financial security or you can have a meaningful life. A combination of both, in my experience, is rare. Many financially secure people I meet are not leading meaningful lives—they are looking for distractions and external meaning. They spend a lot of time rattling around or watching TV."

He said that many of these people have spent years building the financial security they've been told by brokers and mutual fund salesmen that they must have to retire. Then they retire and often don't know what to do with themselves. They may not be happy or find their lives very meaningful, despite their money. "Financial security is a new concept in human history. It's great, but it has its blind side that brokers don't tell you about. It doesn't necessarily lead to a meaningful life, and it can collapse very quickly, as my father and grandfather taught me. An illness, a divorce, a stock market meltdown—any of those could wipe it out overnight. And if you aren't leading a meaningful life and your financial security disappears, what do you have left? Truly blessed are the people with meaningful lives. Add financial security and you're blessed even more. But that's damn rare!"

3

Cutting Back and Simplifying Your Life

Any kind of debt has to be looked at as a mortgage of future income.
—DR. FRED WADDELL, MONEY-MANAGEMENT SPECIALIST

Many of us yearn for a simpler life, with fewer responsibilities and possessions. Such a change can be psychologically liberating; it can also be an important element in reducing your expenses and allowing you to retire early and on less than you believed possible.

Always remember: *cutting expenses increases income*. That may sound simplistic, but consider how many people ignore it. They worry about how to get more money in the form of a raise or an extra job when, in fact, they can often accomplish the same goal just by cutting expenses. You can, in effect, give yourself a raise.

DRAWING THE LINE

Ron and Barb Hofmeister are paragons of simplification. For more than a decade, they have been living full-time on the road in a recreational vehicle. "Everything we own is with us on the road," Barb Hofmeister said from her cell phone somewhere in Minnesota. "We loved it from the beginning. There was such a sense of freedom, a sense of adventure. It simplified life so much."

In 1989, two weeks after Ron Hofmeister, then fifty-six, retired as deputy director of finance for the Michigan Department of Transportation, the couple allowed the lease on their Lansing town house to expire, put most of their possessions in storage, and hit the road. Three years later they sold what they had in storage and have never looked back. They started out in a twenty-four-foot motor home and have graduated to a $200,000, forty-foot diesel-powered model. The Hofmeisters have written three books about their mobile life, including *Movin' On: Living and Traveling Full Time in a Recreational Vehicle* (R & B Publications, 1999). They also have a Web site (www.movinon.net) that, like the book, offers practical advice for those interested in their alternative lifestyle.

Ron Hofmeister said that their motor home gets ten miles a gallon, but that they drive it only seven to ten thousand miles a year. They tow a small Toyota pickup and two bicycles for local travel. They get their mail through a mail-forwarding service in Livingston, Texas. They also "domicile" in Texas, using the address of the mail service, so that's where they vote and maintain driver's licenses. Barb Hofmeister said they had not had any trouble getting medical care on the road. "In fact, we've both had major surgery on the road," she added. The longest they have stayed in one place is seven months. Usually they travel two hundred miles and stay for a week. "We love this life," she said. "Sometimes we think we should settle down, but where would we go? Now we follow the sun and enjoy the best weather all year."

Too Much Stuff

Most people probably don't want to go as far as the Hofmeisters in simplifying their lives. The couple's experience is intended as a starting point for thinking about what you really need in your life. While it's true that we are in some ways defined by our possessions, and there are certain things we would not and should not cast aside, most of us are simply way over the top in this department.

My wife and I have no children. We live in a three-story (plus basement), four-bedroom house. We have two cars, three televisions, three sets of dishes, seven regular telephones, two cellular phones, and two computers—and a garage, basement, and attic filled with stuff we haven't looked at or used in years. An exercise machine serves as a coat rack. We have thousands of photographs and slides, many of which are duplicates of the same people or scenes. We still have our decades-old college textbooks, as well as hundred of books I have squirreled away under the pretense that I'll read them someday.

You get the picture.

Clearly we are candidates for a garage sale. So are many other people, especially those considering retiring. I look forward to eliminating much of this clutter from my life. I might start collecting it again, but at least I will have made a fresh start.

The three most important things to remember are simplify, simplify, simplify. If retirement is a new beginning, let it be so—free of unnecessary baggage from the past. You will feel lighter and your wallet will be heavier.

Take your house.

As chapter 5 will show in detail, for most people their home is their most valuable asset and one of the main keys to retiring sooner and on less money than they thought possible.

Value aside, do you really want or need to retire in a home that is probably much bigger, and more difficult and expensive to maintain, than one or two people need? Moving to a smaller house, whether nearby or farther away, not only frees up the money in your current home but may well free you from a lot of yard work and other home maintenance and worries. There'll probably still be room for children and grandchildren to visit. If not, there are always motels and hotels. After all, you can't be expected to maintain a big, expensive house just so that relatives will have a place to stay a few nights a year.

Whether you plan to buy an existing home or build a new

home, be realistic about how much space one or two people really need. Remember, your goal is to cut some corners so you can retire early. Moving from a four- or five-bedroom house to one with two or three bedrooms is a relatively painless corner to cut.

The True Cost of a Car

If you're serious about trimming back on things, you need to take a hard look at your car or cars. They are a money pit.

First, you'll probably be able to reduce your transportation needs to one car. Not only do you eliminate a car or lease payment, or free up some money if you paid cash, but you also greatly reduce your auto insurance bills, which in some states—like New Jersey, where I live—are considerable.

What will that one car be? Unless there are special tax issues involved, the most expensive thing you can do is buy or lease a new car every two or three years. The least expensive route is to purchase a used car. There is also a middle way: buy a new car and run it until it dies.

One of the problems with a new car is that its rate of depreciation, or decline in value, is much higher during the early life of the vehicle. Buying a used car, or keeping a new car for a long time, allows you to avoid much of that depreciation or minimize it by spreading it out over many years, perhaps ten to twelve. However, a plus to getting a new car every two or three years is that repair costs are reduced because your car is always under warranty.

If you want a demonstration of how really expensive a car is, go to www.Edmunds.com on the Web. Click on the "True Cost to Own," or "TCO," section. There you'll be able to select a car and see the estimated costs of ownership for five years.

Take for instance a 2004 Dodge Intrepid SE full-size, four-door sedan with a 2.7-liter six-cylinder engine. According to Edmunds, the estimated new-car purchase price in New Jersey would be $22,118, including that state's sales tax and fees totaling $1,331. The price of the car without the taxes and fees is

$20,857, a number that will be useful in some later calculations.

The total cost of owning that Intrepid for five years—the TCO—would be $35,370. That includes depreciation, financing, insurance, taxes and fees, fuel, maintenance, and repairs. That works out to an average per-mile cost of 47 cents over the five-year period. (The Internal Revenue Service, however, allows you to deduct only 36 cents a mile when the use of your car is a tax-deductible expense; many companies use the IRS figure to reimburse employees who use their cars for company business.)

Let's look more closely at four of the expense elements in the Edmunds calculations: depreciation, financing, maintenance, and repairs.

Depreciation is the amount by which a car declines in value from its purchase price. As we'll see, most depreciation takes place early on, especially during the first year. In calculating depreciation and resale values, Edmunds assumes that you will drive the car fifteen thousand miles a year, keep it in "clean" condition, and sell it to a private party. If you sell the car to a dealer or use it as a trade-in, it's value would probably be lower.

Financing is the interest expense on a car loan. The amounts in figure 2 are for someone with a good credit rating and assume a down payment of 15 percent and a loan term of sixty months. Edmunds is able to constantly update its Web site to account for the slightest changes in interest rates for loans—and fuel prices—which I obviously can't do here. If you go to the Edmunds Web site you will get a different number for interest charges, fuel costs, and the True Cost to Own, depending on current rates and prices. Financing charges are typically based on the balance due and will decrease over the five years as that balance declines.

Maintenance includes work that needs to be done to your car on a regular basis, like oil changes. It also includes unscheduled things like replacing batteries, brakes, hoses, mufflers, lights, and so on.

Repairs refer to work that must be done on your car but is not covered by the manufacturer's warranty.

Figure 2

Costs of Owning a Typical New Car

Some costs, like maintenance and repair, rise as a car gets older. Others, like depreciation and taxes, are much higher when a car is new. Assuming steady use and a clean driving record, fuel and insurance costs rise gradually with inflation.

	First year	Second year	Third year	Fourth year	Fifth year	Total over five years
Depreciation	$ 6,724	$ 2,171	$ 1,910	$ 1,694	$ 1,519	**$ 14,018**
Repairs	0	0	81	193	284	**558**
Maintenance	346	555	512	1,028	1,393	**3,834**
Taxes and fees	1,331	49	36	36	36	**1,488**
Financing	1,296	1,047	779	489	178	**3,789**
Insurance	1,348	1,368	1,389	1,410	1,431	**6,946**
Fuel	892	919	947	975	1,004	**4,737**
Total	$ 11,937	$ 6,109	$ 5,654	$ 5,825	$ 5,845	**$ 35,370**

Source: Edmunds.com

Both maintenance and repairs—as you might expect—will increase as your car ages.

Putting all the cost elements together, figure 2 shows how Edmunds comes up with the $35,370 that it costs to own a $22,118 car.

As you can see, and probably already know from experience, depreciation is the killer. The value of the Intrepid drops by $6,724 the first year you own it. But in the fifth year, its value will drop by only $1,519. While it's true that maintenance and repairs will rise as a car ages and depreciation drops, as you can see in chart 2 it's not an even match—not even close.

Now imagine that instead of buying that Intrepid new, you buy it when it is three years old. Edmunds estimates its resale value then at $10,052 (the purchase price of the car, without sales tax, minus depreciation). It would have only 45,000 miles on it and the bulk of its depreciation would be in the past, greatly decreasing its per-mile costs. If the car were five years old, with 75,000 miles on it, you could pick it up for $6,839. By then, depreciation would have tapered way off and the per-mile costs would be even less. Most modern cars can easily go 100,000 miles or more without serious mechanical problems. If you buy the car with 75,000 miles on it, you can reasonably expect to drive it another 30,000 miles, or two years, without a serious breakdown. Now look back at figure 2. The price of the five-year-old car—$6,839—that you're going to drive for two years, or perhaps longer, *is $2,056 less than the depreciation alone on a new Intrepid for just the first two years!*

If you drive that five-year-old car longer than two years, the per-mile costs gets less and less the longer you drive it—to a point. That point is when repairs get too expensive. More about that later.

I have some friends who are very good at buying used cars. They often wind up with some very fancy automobiles—ten-year-old BMWs and the like—for less than the price of a new subcompact.

Because I have never been very skillful or lucky at buying used cars, I have adopted the middle way: buying a new car and running it as long as possible. While you will take the initial hit on depreciation, keeping the car long enough—ten years or so—will spread the loss over enough years so that it is much less painful than buying a new car every three years or so. Remember, most of the depreciation occurs in the first three years—and especially the first year—of owning a new car. Note that the five-year depreciation total on a new Intrepid is $14,018, with the drop in the fifth year being only $1,519. That averages out to a bit over $2,800 a year. If you keep the car for ten years—and even assume that at that point it's worth zero—the per-year average drops to $2,086. If you keep it twelve years, that average declines to $1,738. By keeping a car twelve years instead of three, you have cut the annual depreciation cost to $1,738 from $2,800.

Back to repairs. They will climb as a car gets older. The trick is to know when to stop—both in terms of expense and inconvenience.

In 1991, I bought a new Saab 900 and drove it for eleven years, putting close to 150,000 miles on its odometer. The price of the car, without sales tax, was $18,300. My per-year depreciation cost worked out to $1,663. Actually, it was less than that, but for our purposes I'm assuming that the value of the car was zero at the end.

During the last three years that I owned the car, I had to have some repair work done, but it never ran more than $1,500 a year. Each time I had a $500 or $600 repair bill, I would remind myself that this amount was less than just two monthly car payments on a new car. Finally, however, the Saab needed some extensive transmission work that was going to cost several thousand dollars. Plus, the frequency of repairs was becoming an inconvenience. I decided it was time to get rid of the car, which I donated to a charity in exchange for a tax deduction. My decision was not the result of any magic formula, just my own sense of timing based on expense and inconvenience.

Jeff Brown is a personal finance columnist for the *Philadelphia Inquirer*. He admits to having a bee in his bonnet on the subject of cars and how much they cost. In his column, he has complained that "too many people buy new cars to keep up with the Joneses," adding that "over a lifetime of car ownership, the cost can be enormous—forcing many serial new-car buyers to delay retirement for years."

He expanded on this in an interview. "An awful lot of our car culture is based on the idea of showing off with a fancy and expensive new car," he said. "If that really, really matters to you and is part of what makes you happy, I guess you've got to spend money for it." Otherwise, he advocates buying a used car or keeping a new one for as long as possible. "While I don't think you should live a life of want and be miserable or inconvenienced, I do think you ought to look very closely at value and what really matters to you," he continued. "It's wonderful to have a new Mercedes, but I wouldn't get pleasure from it worth the additional ten or twenty thousand dollars it would cost. Especially as you get older and are perhaps looking to retire and fulfill a dream. If instead of a Mercedes you bought a used car, it could mean retiring earlier and easier. And you'd still be driving a decent car. I'm not talking about driving an old beater down the road trailing smoke and parts. There are some awfully good used cars out there, like those that have just come off lease. I'm talking about a car that still has eighty percent of its life in it, but has lost fifty to sixty percent of its cost. It's value, a good deal."

For those who want to keep a car until it dies, he stresses the importance of regular maintenance: "The trick really is good maintenance. Cars are so much better made now than they used to be. Sure, repairs increase as a car gets older, but a car that's been fairly well maintained ought to run to a hundred thousand miles before it needs major repairs." He says he considers a major repair something that requires work "deep in the heart of a transmission or engine and involves things like pistons or crankshafts. If you have to replace things that hang on the outside of the engine—alternators and pumps, for instance—to me those are maintenance items like tires and brakes. But a major repair is a serious issue and may be the point at which you decide it's no longer worth it. My rule of thumb is that when the annual maintenance costs get close to what the payments would be on a new car, then you're probably paying too much for maintenance and it might be time for a new car. But short of that it's just a matter of comparing what it costs to maintain and what it costs to buy new. Of course, you have to factor in the headache value of putting up with possible breakdowns and inconvenience."

There is yet another school of thought on cars that recommends making major repairs—even if they are expensive—and getting a second or third life out of a vehicle. This is probably best exemplified by James McCain, the retired professor in chapter 2. His Volkswagen Beetle had a twice-rebuilt engine and 400,000 miles on the odometer before he finally sold it.

Although admittedly not for everyone, this method of coping with transportation is not without its merits. Suppose you spend, say, $5,000 to $7,000 to rebuild a car's engine and transmission plus other items that may need more than routine maintenance.

That's pretty cheap compared to the $20,000 you would spend for a new car. The rebuilt one might run nearly as long as the new one before needing major work.

Wherever you come down on the car issue, there's no argument that cars are an expensive, if necessary, component of our modern life. The most expensive way of all is to lease or buy a new car every two or three years. If that's been your practice, it's a great place to start cutting expenses so you can retire on less than the "experts" say.

It's Only a Dollar

One of my pet peeves about money is how fast the little things can add up. Perhaps during your workweek you buy a couple of cans of cola or bottles of water a day from a machine or a deli that charges $1 each for them. That's $10 a week, or $520 a year. If you buy a case of water or soda from a discount store, the per-item price drops to about 25 cents. Stick a couple of bottles or cans in your bag or briefcase and save $1.50 a day, or 7.50 a week—or, $390 a year.

Let's take this a step further. If you took that $7.50 a week, put it aside, and each month put the $30 you would have accumulated into some type of savings or investment earning 6.5 percent, in ten years you would have more than $5,000. In twenty years, you would have more than $14,000! And you haven't given up anything.

Do you spend $10 a day on lunch? Bring your lunch for a cost, say, of $2 and save the $8 difference. That's $40 a week you could invest. In ten years you would be almost $27,000 richer; in twenty years, almost $77,000! Again, you haven't given up anything. In fact, you may have gained in the health department because the food you bring from home is likely to be better for you than what you buy in a restaurant or over a lunch counter.

You can also look at this as money you don't have to spend when you're retired. Or, if for you retirement means continuing to work on your own terms or at something you've always dreamed of, just cutting back on expenses for lunch and drinks either before or after you "retire" can make your goal that much more possible.

These calculations don't take inflation or taxes into account, but the point is clear and you should think about it the next time you casually drop a few bucks on something you could get cheaper elsewhere or easily do without.

Lotteries are another pet peeve. Sure, there's no harm buying a $1 lottery ticket now and then when the jackpot gets huge. But I used to work with a man who every week would spend $30 on lottery tickets. He used to laugh when I pointed out that the odds of winning a state lottery were astronomical. "Well, somebody has to win," he would shrug. I finally got his attention when I pointed out that if he invested that $30 a week, or $120 a month, for thirty years at 6.5 percent interest, he would have almost $130,000. He said he had a friend who spent $100 a week on lottery tickets. Well, $400 a month for thirty years at 6.5 percent would come to more than $425,000! My workmate was astounded. I don't know if he stopped playing the lottery, but I'm sure these calculations were in the back of his mind every time he bought a ticket.

The Whopper Test

Jeff Brown, the *Philadelphia Inquirer* columnist, looks at the issue of spending from another angle. In one of his columns, he asks if you would be so quick to buy a can of Coke from a machine if, instead of $1, the price was $5. That's what he figures $1 today, if invested at 8.38 percent a year, will be worth in twenty years. He calls the difference "lost investment earnings."

While I have used 6.5 percent, he used 8.38 percent, partly to get the final number to be exactly $5. He also thinks 8.38 percent is on the conservative side, compared with twenty-year market returns of 10 to 12 percent. I felt more comfortable using 6.5 percent for my calculations because there have been long periods when the market has languished; between 1968 and 1978, for example, it lost

45 percent of its value. Historically, the market has returned about 7 percent. And there are plenty of economists who predict weak returns for the next twenty years. But if you're a market bull, that can of soda looks even more expensive.

But what's important here is the concept, not the exact numbers. You can save a lot of money, or cut your expenses dramatically, if you are willing to pay attention to the little things that add up to big money over time.

In one of his columns, Jeff has described what he calls the "Whopper Test" for spending money. For instance, if you pay $40 for a meal, is it ten times better than a Burger King Whopper with cheese? If not, Jeff says, it fails his Whopper Test. What Jeff is getting at is your sense of value. After you spend money for something, do you honestly feel you got good value? For me, most expensive restaurant meals fail this test. And I almost never feel I get value for an expensive hotel or motel room, where I usually just sleep for a few hours. Then again, some people would be aghast at what I spend for bicycles and related equipment.

Some expenditures, of course, pass his Whopper Test more easily than others. Home repairs, for instance, usually pass because you'll probably get some of that money back when you sell your home. A fancy car may or may not pass, depending on your personal situation and how much your ego is linked to what you drive.

You need to be flexible. As Jeff put it in his Whopper Test column: "Over time, of course, one's sense of value evolves, so it pays to readminister the Whopper Test once in a while. As a cost-saving move, I used to change the oil in my cars myself. Then a day came when I decided it really was worth 10 or 15 bucks to avoid climbing under there and getting that stuff in my face." He continued: "In the same way, I've decided it's worth $4 to take my pickup to the car wash. But only in the winter. In the warm months, I scrub it myself."

Where to draw the line on all this is, naturally, up to your individual preferences and tolerances and your sense of value. In most of our lives, however, there's a lot of financial slack that can be taken up with minimal change. The payoff can be early retirement.

THE PLASTIC TRAP AND OTHER DEBT

Spending too much becomes even more critical if you're doing it on credit. Relax. Even though it's hard to overstate the problem, this is not another lecture on the danger of credit card debt. You know about that already. This is just a reminder that such debt can imperil your retirement plans.

Fred Waddell, the money-management specialist who trains financial counselors, always includes in his seminars a section on eliminating deficits, or "reducing negative cash flow." In simple terms, this means retiring with as little debt as possible—preferably none. "Any kind of debt has to be looked at as a mortgage of future income," Waddell said. "It is a claim against future income. It becomes very difficult to calculate how much you're going to live on in retirement if the amount of money you're using in your calculations is not really yours but belongs to your creditors."

He says as you approach retirement you should reduce your outstanding debt to as close to zero as possible. All debt is not created equal, however. Credit card debt and debt for a depreciating asset, like a car, should be paid off first, starting with the debt that carries the highest interest. Some mortgage debt may be tolerable because the underlying asset, a house, is presumably appreciating in value, effectively reducing the interest costs. "Some advisers say pay off all debt, including mortgage debt," Waddell said. "I would say pay off the mortgage debt if possible. But certainly pay off all other debt like credit cards and car loans. If you're paying fourteen to seventeen percent interest on credit card debt and you pay that off, it's like earning fourteen to seventeen percent on your money."

If there were no early-withdrawal penalties involved, would he advise dipping into retirement savings to pay off such debt? "Yes," was his immediate reply. "And that's a no-brainer now that savings are earning one or two percent and credit cards are charging up to eighteen percent, and sometimes more, on balances." He also advises that as you approach retirement, you consider making prepayments on your mortgage. "I did this and it worked out pretty well," he said. "All my investments were in stocks, so I looked on my mortgage prepayments as the missing bond portion of my portfolio." The result of mortgage prepayments can be dramatic, even if you are close to having your house paid for.

For instance, let's assume that in January 1980 you signed a $250,000 home mortgage with a 7 percent thirty-year fixed-rate loan. That means if you made the regular monthly payments of $1,663.26 for thirty years, or 360 months, your house would be paid for in January 2010. But if in January 2003 you started paying an extra $500 a month on the mortgage, you would pay the loan off one year and eleven months sooner (in February 2008) and save $8,770.66 in interest.

Now let's assume that with this same mortgage, you had decided to start making those $500-a-month prepayments in January 1990. That would have cut seven years and eight months off your loan and your house would have been paid for in May 2002. Interest saved: $78,555.75.

There are several good mortgage calculators on the Web where you can plug in the numbers to make them fit your particular situation. My favorite, and the one I used for these calculations, is on the Bloomberg Web site (www.bloomberg.com). Prepayment is not limited to mortgages, of course. It works with credit card bills too. However you do it, getting rid of debt will certainly make your retirement easier and will probably allow it to happen sooner. Remember, when you reduce debt—or cut other expenses—you increase income.

A Special Invitation (to Anyone)

Like most of us, Ann Hamman—who died in June 2003 at age ninety-five—was deluged with mail offering "preapproved" credit cards and various lines of credit from banks and financial services companies, large and small. Gold cards, platinum cards, titanium cards. Credit lines of as much as $100,000. During the final few years of her life, however, Ann Hamman never saw these offers. That is because she lived in an assisted-living residence in Homestead, Florida. She suffered from memory problems and needed help with daily activities; she was unable to prepare meals or manage a bank account. Her mail went to her son, Henry Hamman, who lives nearby in Miami. Hamman, who had his mother's power of attorney, said he was appalled at the mail solicitations she received. "When you market indiscriminately to the elderly and the susceptible, I think it's pretty reprehensible," he said. "This is the financial equivalent of handing a loaded gun to a kid."

He is particularly angry about a check his mother received from Household Bank in Las Vegas, a subsidiary of Household International. The check was for $1,500.02. All Ann Hamman had to do was endorse it and, presto, the money would be hers—along with a legal obligation to repay the loan in monthly installments of $55.72 for forty-eight months. That means that she would repay $2,674.56, which translates to an annual interest rate of 31.945 percent. "If this check had fallen into her hands, it's entirely conceivable that she might have used it and not really known what she was doing," Hamman said.

A spokeswoman for Household International, which is based in Prospect Heights, Illinois, said her company did not specifically single out older people for such solicitations. She agreed that the 31.945 percent rate offered to Ann Hamman was "stunning."

Henry Hamman was also puzzled that many of the offers cited his mother's excellent credit history as a reason for offering her up to $100,000 of credit. "She didn't have any credit," he said. "She had no assets other than her pension and Social Security and hadn't owned a home since the 1960s. She even got credit offers beyond the grave, including thirty thousand dollars for an automobile loan. Either there was a credit report mix-up or this is the biggest bunch of hooey I've ever seen." A spokeswoman in Washington for the American Bankers Association, a lobbying group, said that members "look at creditworthiness" before making credit card offers.

Ann Hamman grew up in Oklahoma and during World War II was a lieutenant in the Women's Army Corps, serving in Italy and Algeria. She later worked in Indiana as a consumer education agent and as a food editor at the *Evansville Courier*. After retiring, she served in the Peace Corps in Belize for two years. "She was always a very independent person who stood up for folks who couldn't stand up for themselves," her son said. "These credit offers would have upset her because of the damage they can do to people who aren't financially sophisticated." The seemingly personal solicitations can also prove seductive to the psychologically vulnerable. Ann Hamman was lucky that she had her son to look out for her in these matters. Many older people who are on their own—especially if they are homebound, lonely, or confused—can easily fall victim to such practices that, while not illegal, are certainly questionable.

Travis B. Plunkett, the legislative director of the Consumer Federation of America, based in Washington, D.C., said "indiscriminate and reckless marketing" had become the rule in the credit card industry, which mails out billions of solicitations each year. "Their business model, the way they profit, is to make risky loans to people who often don't have the financial skills to know whether it's right or not," he added. "They'll give a credit card to anything that moves."

Consider the case involving the late Doug X. Ping. Doug was a Shar-Pei who was struck by a car and killed in 1994, when he was five. Gordon Krelove, the dog's owner, who had brought the pet to the United States from China, later put Doug's name on some random consumer survey. Soon, Doug received a solicitation from First USA Bank in Wilmington, Delaware, for a National Geographic Society platinum MasterCard with a "solid line of credit" of up to $100,000.

A spokesman for First USA Bank, which is a member of the banking association and a subsidiary of Bank One, said, "We make every effort to ensure that the offers we mail out go to credit-eligible adults."

If you're not a dog, you can take some steps to limit the number of mail solicitations you receive. For a $5 fee, the Web site of the Direct Marketing Association (www.the-dma.org/consumers) allows you to remove your name from its members' mailing lists. The same service is free if you write to an address provided on the Web site. There is also an automated toll-free number (888-567-8688) that allows you to remove your name from mailing lists provided by the big credit-reporting agencies. But perhaps the best advice on dealing with credit solicitations comes from James A. Guest, the president of Consumers Union, based in Yonkers, New York. "Just throw the stuff in the trash," he said.

LIFE INSURANCE

A lot of people in their fifties are perplexed about life insurance. If they have term insurance, the premiums are probably getting too expensive; if they have universal life that is linked to interest rates, they may be facing higher premiums to maintain coverage. In reality, life insurance is a good place for many people with sufficient assets to cut expenses. They simply may be paying for something they don't really need.

Deena Katz, the financial adviser in Coral Gables, Florida, points out that life insurance "manages risks," adding: "You have it to replace your income or for some specific need for your family when you're not there. If you don't have that need, you don't need the insurance. If you're not providing for your family after your death—say your kids are grown and out on their own—and you're retired with other assets to provide for your spouse, there's no risk to manage."

She advises people in this situation to cancel or cash in their life insurance policies and put the monthly premiums into long-term care insurance instead. But consult a financial adviser first; if your policy has cash value, you may be able to shelter the proceeds from current taxes.

4

Where Will You Live?

*We were looking for a way to live more simply in jobs that are
more rewarding, that bring value to society and ourselves.*
—KENDRA GOLDEN

Late in 2001, Bill and Donna Taaffe learned that the annual taxes
on their ninety-three-year-old home in Maplewood, New Jersey, a
suburb of New York, would nearly double to $15,800 ($1,317 a
month) in the coming year from $8,200 ($683 a month) because of
a reassessment. In addition, the increase was retroactive to the
beginning of 2001, which meant they owed a lump-sum payment of
about $8,000 in addition to the future monthly increase. The Taaffes
fought back and eventually succeeded in getting the increase lowered to $13,500, or $1,125 a month. The retroactive payment was
reduced to $5,500. "But it was a huge hit," Bill Taaffe said. "It
helped deplete our savings pretty fast. That increase made things
financially very tight for us. It was almost impossible to make it on
our salaries." Bill Taaffe was a sports editor at the *New York Times*
for ten years, and, before that, a writer for *Sports Illustrated*; Donna
Taaffe worked for a nonprofit organization in New Jersey.

By the next summer, the property taxes were increased again

and the couple—he was fifty-nine and she was fifty-eight—decided they had had it. "We felt like every dollar we made we were just pouring into the house," Bill Taaffe said. "We were barely keeping our heads above water and had all that stress and anxiety. It just didn't make any sense."

"THE CAT BY THE TAIL"

The Taaffes sold their home in Maplewood, quit their jobs, and moved with their adopted nine-year-old son to Henderson, Nevada, a suburb of Las Vegas, where Donna's cousin—"more like a sister," according to Bill—had moved with her family two years earlier. With the profit from the sale of their house in New Jersey the Taaffes were able to pay cash for a modern home they liked better than their old one and install a swimming pool and Jacuzzi.

Although Bill continues to work—as a freelance writer, mainly of books—he says what he did amounts to a retirement of sorts. "I guess it was a kind of a segue into retirement," he said. "I like doing things on my own terms. That commute into New York was a grind that just got old. But I'm probably never going to fully retire. I'm always going to keep my hand in."

The experience of Bill and Donna Taaffe is worth examining in some detail for two reasons. First, their unorthodox "retirement" is typical of how many baby boomers say they plan to leave their traditional jobs. Second, theirs is a classic example of the importance of where you retire—it is a huge factor in how well you can live and, perhaps, whether you can retire earlier.

Bill estimates that by moving to Nevada, he and his wife cut their expenses by more than half; the property taxes on their new home, for instance, are $1,500 *a year*. And that's in addition to living mortgage-free. While they will face college expenses for their son in a few years, Bill said they had already provided for that in their savings.

Comparing Places

Their experience is quantified by www.BestPlaces.net and www. RetirementLiving.com, two Web sites mentioned in chapter 2. Since Bill Taaffe commuted into New York City, let's compare the metro areas first. According to www.BestPlaces.net, it is 55.2 percent cheaper to live in the Las Vegas area than in New York. In other words, a $44,800 salary in Las Vegas would go as far as a $100,000 salary in New York. (Remember, that comparison assumes comparable expenses *and a mortgage payment*.) A home that would cost $341,330 in New York would be priced at $123,120 in Las Vegas. The overall cost-of-living index, with 100 being the national average, is 193.4 in New York and 108 in Las Vegas.

Www.BestPlaces.net allows you to compare smaller cities and towns. Putting Maplewood and Henderson side by side is equally jarring. The median cost of a home in Maplewood is $241,120; in Henderson, it's $144,770. Maplewood's property tax rate per $1,000 of assessed valuation is listed at $26.30, compared with $10.20 in Henderson; the national average is $16.43. The Web site also allows you to compare other factors, like people and population, the economy, health, crime, education, climate, and transportation.

Www.RetirementLiving.com points out that Nevada is one of nine states with no personal income tax, so there is no tax on retirement income. In addition, homeowners who are at least sixty-two years old and earn $23,156 a year or less are eligible for a rebate of up to $500 or 90 percent of their property taxes. The main reason that taxes are low in Nevada, of course, is casino gambling and the tourists and conventions it attracts. All this money from outsiders generates taxes and other benefits that help keep residents' taxes low. "Henderson overlooks Las Vegas and we can see planes coming in over the valley to land," Bill Taaffe said. "My wife's cousin's husband sometimes says, 'Here comes another planeload of people to pay our taxes.' If you don't gamble, you kind of have the cat by the tail here."

. . .

Bill and Donna Taaffe were very deliberate in their decision to move. "We came to the conclusion that we had a choice," Bill Taaffe said. "If I continued working in New York, we would have to move to a smaller house in Maplewood or further out on the train line to a cheaper place with a longer commute. Then in eight years when our son went to college, we would retire and move again. We decided this was crazy. Why not move once, to an area of the country where we knew we could make a go of it? I had a book deal and I knew I could do other books after that. I knew there were all sorts of projects I could do on my own. It was like a zero-sum game. We wanted to move somewhere where if we didn't do anything for the next six years until we were eligible for Social Security, we could still make it. We knew what our house was worth and what we could buy a house for in Nevada."

Their New Jersey house sold in one day—without the services of a real estate agent, so they pocketed the 6 percent commission. They had paid $252,000 for the four-bedroom home in 1996. They sold it for $465,000. After paying off the balance of their mortgage, they walked away with about $250,000. "We were attracted to Nevada because we had been there to visit Donna's cousin in Henderson," Bill said. "We had also lived for two years in Colorado and loved the West. Plus, I knew different parts of the country from work-related travel."

In August 2002, they moved to Henderson and lived with Donna's cousin for several weeks until they bought a home. "We found a new home for a fraction of what we were spending in New Jersey, where our house had all sorts of problems and constantly needed fixing," Bill continued. They paid $184,000 for the Nevada house and put another $30,000 into some additions they wanted, including the pool and Jacuzzi. "In retrospect, the decision was a no-brainer. By moving out here, we have been able to live more comfortably and work at our own pace. Plus, we're living in a place and a home we really like. Our new house has four bedrooms, three baths, and is all on one level, a feature we find very comfortable. Everything out here is less expensive. Prescriptions, restaurants, entertainment, car repairs—you name it. If you don't gamble, you can really make out at the casinos where they have good food at incredible prices. Also, despite being one of the fastest-growing areas in the country, the traffic hassle here is about twenty-five percent of what it was in the New York area. Donna will eventually return to work, probably freelancing, and that will give us another revenue stream. But owning our home free and clear—no mortgage payment—makes a big difference."

The Taaffes' Health Insurance

One wrinkle in the Taaffes' move was health insurance. Bill would have had to work for three more years to formally retire from the *New York Times* and have retirement health benefits. "We just didn't want to struggle for three more years," he said. "In addition, we thought it would be much easier for our son to move at nine than at twelve or thirteen. And it's worked out okay for him; he likes it out here." So he continued his company health insurance under a federal plan called COBRA (short for Consolidated Omnibus Budget Reconciliation Act of 1985) that allows participants who leave a job to extend—at their own expense—their health insurance benefits for eighteen months. The price can be hefty. For the Taaffes, it's about $1,000 a month.

"But we took that expense into account," Bill said. "We know when the eighteen months are up, we'll have to go to the open market and seek family health plans. But I think by the time we get to that point, it'll be fine. We'll take it in stride." (Chapter 6 looks at some health insurance options for people in the same situation as the Taaffes.)

...

The Taaffes were lucky in that they had relatives in Henderson and knew the area somewhat from previous visits. It can be difficult to pull up roots, leave an area you know and where you have friends and perhaps family, and move to somewhere new. "We were a little worried about Nevada and Las Vegas because of their reputation for being a transient community," Bill said. "That was, and still is to some extent, a negative in my mind. But we haven't really felt a lack of community here. Henderson is family-oriented and the schools are good. It's really not part of the glitz of Las Vegas."

DECISIONS, DECISIONS

Although most surveys indicate that the majority of people want to stay put when they retire, those annual "Best Places" articles in personal finance magazines are always a big hit.

I expect there is something of a disconnect between people's responses to these surveys and reality. As mentioned in chapter 2, I wonder if the answers to these survey questions would be different if they explained that staying put may mean you can't retire as early as you might like.

I don't mean to play down the importance of family, friends, community, or one's sense of place. But retiring to a cheaper area doesn't necessarily mean giving up all these things. We live in such a mobile society that most of us have friends and relatives spread across the country. Many of us are living where we are—and maintaining our expensive lifestyles—because of our jobs, not because of family or friends or other ties. The Taaffes, for instance, actually moved closer to some family members when they moved to the Las Vegas area.

Richard E. Mayer, an independent financial consultant in Mineola, New York, agrees. "The baby boomers and their families are spread out all over the place, so retiring to be near family or friends is less of an issue," he said.

If your goal is to retire early, where you decide to live is an extremely important and difficult decision. You do not want to wind up in a place where you are not happy and then quickly make another move.

It's important to do research at Web sites like www.Best Places.net and www.RetirementLiving.com. It's even more important to vacation in places where you think you might want to retire—and not just at the best times of the year. Go to Arizona or Florida in the summer. Check Maine or Colorado in the winter. Talk to residents and look carefully at the local newspaper. Better yet, if you have the time and money, rent an apartment and live in your chosen town for a few months to really get a feel for the place.

In the early 1990s, Joseph and Joyce Ensminger moved from their home state of Kansas to Green Valley, Arizona, a retirement community about twenty miles south of Tucson. They went there because Joseph Ensminger, now ninety-three, had been hospitalized with pneumonia, and they were seeking a warmer and drier climate.

In 1999 they moved back.

"Green Valley is a lovely place, but I missed my children and family," Joyce Ensminger, seventy-eight, said. "After all, family is everything." She conceded that she wanted to return more than her husband and that he went along to please her. "Joe had recently had a serious operation, and he felt a little mortal," she said. "He wanted to know that I was all settled before something happened to him."

The Ensmingers are not alone. Many retirees move to another part of the country, then decide to return to where they had lived and worked most of their lives. Usually they long to be closer to family members, often because of failing health or the death of a spouse. Sometimes, they fail to make new friends or otherwise decide that they don't like their new environment as much as they thought. Arizona or Florida can be wonderful in February; August is another story.

Precise figures are difficult to come by, but Charles F. Longino Jr., a gerontologist at Wake Forest University in Winston-Salem, North Carolina, uses census data to estimate that about 5 percent of retirees actually move to another state. Of that share, as many as 10 percent may eventually return. According to the most recent available data, 104,000 people over sixty years old moved from New York to Florida between 1985 and 1990, while 9,000 moved from Florida to New York.

For the Ensmingers and others like them, the trade-offs were not worth it. Joseph Ensminger is a retired sports referee and sales manager for a safety-glass maker. Joyce Ensminger is a retired public school administrative assistant. They have both been married before, and between them have six children, fifteen grandchildren, and three great-grandchildren. They sold their Arizona home and built a new house in Overland Park, Kansas, a suburb of Kansas City.

For Joseph Ensminger, his wife's considerations outweighed the Sun Belt's virtues. "However, in many ways Arizona was ideal for me—you wake up every morning and the sun is shining. But we were twelve hundred miles from Kansas City. One family member had been out once and another twice. To see our family we had to travel there. Now we're back with people we know."

Many retirees who are tempted to leave their new locales, however, decide to remain. A second move can be stressful—and expensive. If you live in an area that has been overdeveloped, you may have trouble selling your home. It took the Ensmingers, for example, several months to sell their Green Valley house; meanwhile, their money was tied up. There are also real estate commissions, moving expenses, and a myriad of incidental costs. That second move can wind up costing tens of thousands of dollars.

In the mid-1990s, Jean S. Beals, eighty-two, moved to Naples, Florida, from Mount Holly, New Jersey. A retired bank teller, she has been a widow since 1981. Once, during a trip back to New Jersey, she considered returning. "I got homesick," she said. "I thought maybe I shouldn't have moved. I missed my friends and my church." But Beals had something to draw her back to Florida that many retirees there lack: a daughter in Naples and a son in Sarasota. "So I finally decided no," she said. "I have a lovely place in Florida, and I don't like cold weather anymore. Plus my children are near me. It's too stressful for me to move now."

Trendy Has Its Price

I'm always a bit leery of those "Best Places" lists that appear in magazines. For one thing, the lists are usually different each year in *the same magazine.* How can a town be number one or two one year and not even on the list the next? This suggests a certain manufactured ranking. Second, as soon as a town shows up on one of these lists, you can be certain property values will soon start to rise. Many of the features that made the town attractive will melt away as popularity pushes up its population and degrades its services and attractive features. Santa Fe, New Mexico, is a good example of this. Always popular with tourists, the city has become a trendy retirement destination over the last couple of decades and homes have soared in value. A lot of people from Southern California, their bank accounts fat from selling homes whose value skyrocketed in the 1980s and 1990s, have moved to Santa Fe and bid up property prices. Throw in a few Hollywood celebrities who buy second homes, and the mix has produced a lot of overpriced property. And—although modest by the standards of Los Angeles and New York—traffic and related congestion have taken their toll on the city's quality of life.

One solution is to use those magazine articles as a guide to an area rather than a specific town or city. If you like Santa Fe, for instance, but find it a bit rich for your budget, look sixty-five miles east at Las Vegas, New Mexico. If you use the comparisons provided by www.BestPlaces.net, you'll find that the climate and terrain are similar; the comfort index for both is a high 66, compared with the national average of 34. However, the air quality in Las Vegas is twice as good as that in Santa Fe, and the population of Las Vegas is only about a quarter of Santa Fe's 65,000.

As might be expected from its popularity as a retirement haven, the median age of Santa Fe residents is forty, while in Las Vegas it's thirty. Perhaps the most telling statistic www.Best Places.net offers about the relative trendiness (and cost of living) of the two cities is that Santa Fe has several Starbucks coffee shops; Las Vegas has none. But trendy has its price. The home cost index, which includes rentals, is 93.5 in Las Vegas and 256.9 in Santa Fe; this index is based on a national average of 100. The differences in home prices is even more striking. The median home cost in the United States is $146,102. In Las Vegas, New Mexico, it is $108,750, while in Santa Fe it is $298,840. The overall cost-of-living index—again, with the national average at 100—is 101.6 in Las Vegas and 155.3 in Santa Fe. This means it costs 50 percent more to live in Santa Fe than Las Vegas.

However, as is often the case, the flip side of an area with a lower cost of living is lower incomes. This is the case in Las Vegas, where average per-capita income is $11,050 a year and average annual household income is $25,943; the same figures for Santa Fe are $26,206 and $42,652, respectively. The national averages are $21,658 and $44,958. As might be expected, the unemployment rate in Las Vegas is 6.8 percent, compared with 2.9 percent in Santa Fe, which has a lot of tourism-related jobs. Also, certain categories of crimes are higher in Las Vegas than in Santa Fe or the national average.

Las Vegas certainly does not have the amenities and shopping of Santa Fe. However, it takes less than an hour to drive to Santa Fe on Interstate 25. So traveling there for dinner or to attend a cultural event is relatively easy.

While there are many reasons why New Mexico is an attractive state, Tom Wetzel of www.RetirementLiving.com points out that the state's tax laws can be particularly tough on the retired. New Mexico is one of six states he cites that have relatively high top-tax brackets and fully tax most retirement income. The other five are California, Montana, Nebraska, North Dakota, and Vermont.

Let's look next door at Arizona, which has a friendlier tax structure for retirees. Social Security benefits, for example, are exempt from state taxes. Keeping with the idea of finding more affordable places near the "Best Places," let's use data from www.Best Places. net and consider Scottsdale and Tempe—both part of the sprawling Phoenix metropolitan area.

Upscale Scottsdale is often cited in lists of good places to retire, and for excellent reasons. It has a great climate, especially in the winter, with an average of 295 sunny days a year. It has many first-rate restaurants, hotels, golf courses, and other amenities, but like Santa Fe, it has become expensive as it has become popular. Nearby Tempe, of course, has an identical climate. While it's not as posh, it is a pleasant and comfortable city that is home to Arizona State University.

But for the budget-minded who want to live in this area, Tempe's biggest advantage is the price of housing. It's home cost index is 113, a bit above the national average of 100, while Scottsdale's is 168.2. The median price of a house in Tempe is $131,530, well below the nation's $146,102; Scottsdale's median home price is $195,620.

The overall cost-of-living index, based on a national average of 100, is 109.6 for Tempe and 127.8 for Scottsdale. Average annual per-capita income in Tempe is $23,020, compared with the national average of $21,658; household income is $42,617, compared with the national average of $44,958. For Scottsdale, per-capita income is $37,656 and household is $51,334.

The population of Scottsdale is about 170,000; Tempe, 193,000. The median age of Scottsdale residents is 39.2; for Tempe, it's 29.7—not unexpected given Scottsdale's popularity with retirees.

If you like the Phoenix area, but can't afford Scottsdale, Tempe is clearly a reasonable alternative. You can zip over to Scottsdale as often as you like.

These comparisons are easy to do on your own. All you need is a good map and Internet access.

Let's look at one more example, this time in Florida.

Naples, with a population of about 20,000 on the Gulf Coast of South Florida, is often mentioned as a top retirement spot. Like Scottsdale in Arizona, it's very nice. Also like Scottsdale, it's pricey.

However, about thirty-five miles to the north—between Sanibel Island and Fort Myers—is Cape Coral, with a population of about 100,000. Like Tempe, Cape Coral's big advantage is lower housing prices. The median price of a home there is $101,330, compared with $164,390 in Naples and the nationwide $146,102. The housing cost index, which includes rentals, is 81.7 for Cape Coral and 141.3 for Naples, compared with the national average of 100.

Not surprisingly, the median age in Naples is sixty, while in Cape Coral it's forty-one. The average per-capita income in Cape Coral is $21,626, almost the same as the nation's $21,658. For Naples, it's $66,800. Household income in Naples is $67,919, compared with $39,314 in Cape Coral and $44,958 nationwide.

A plus no matter where you live in Florida: like Nevada, it is one of the nine states with no personal income tax.

Per-Mile Costs

For more evidence of the wide variations in costs of living around the country, consider a 2003 study by Runzheimer International (www.runzheimer.com), a big management consulting firm, on automobile service and maintenance expenses. The firm found that it costs almost twice as much to maintain a car in San Francisco as it does in Bismarck, North Dakota. The per-mile costs were based on a typical intermediate-size vehicle represented by a 2003 Ford Taurus SEL sedan driven fifteen thousand miles a year and retained for four years. Maintenance expenses include normal and preventive procedures like oil changes, lubrication, and brake and exhaust system inspections: the stuff you're supposed to do according to your car's service manual. They do not include fuel, insurance, tires, or the costs of the car itself. Driving conditions were taken into consideration to develop "typical" and "severe" maintenance per-mile values. "The cost to own and operate your vehicle varies considerably based on driving territory, and maintenance is just one example," said Ted Lewin, a vehicle cost specialist with Runzheimer. "Fuel, vehicle insurance, and license and registration fees are other variables that determine total cost."

Here are the cities Runzheimer found to be the most expensive, along with the per-mile maintenance costs for each:

San Francisco	6.79 cents
New York City	6.38 cents
Hempstead (Long Island)	5.62 cents
Honolulu	5.49 cents
Chicago	5.21 cents
Miami	5.17 cents
Newark, New Jersey	5.13 cents
St. Louis	5.13 cents
Stamford, Connecticut	5.09 cents
Sacramento, California	5.01 cents
Seattle	5.01 cents

Here are the least expensive cities:

Bismarck, North Dakota	3.56 cents
Casper, Wyoming	3.64 cents
Richmond, Virginia	3.68 cents
Lubbock, Texas	3.76 cents
Billings, Montana	3.80 cents
Omaha, Nebraska	3.80 cents
Henderson, Kentucky	3.88 cents
Jackson, Mississippi	3.88 cents

Burlington, Vermont	3.92 cents
Evansville, Indiana	3.92 cents
Montgomery, Alabama	3.92 cents
Portland, Maine	3.92 cents

Dream Towns

Despite my concern about "Best Places" articles in magazines, there is one I would like to mention because of its link to baby boomers. The May–June 2003 issue of *AARP The Magazine* lists fifteen top "dream towns" for boomers that it says show this generation once again breaking the rules by rejecting traditional retirement communities and opting for places with appealing cultural and recreational lifestyles. The magazine says the boomers want places with a "youthful vibe," great medical facilities, and sophisticated restaurants. As pointed out in chapter 2, many boomers will continue working, but on their own terms. This is reinforced by the magazine's survey, which says the boomers will first pick a place they like and then look for a job or become an entrepreneur, rather than follow a job to a place.

Here are the boomers' choices, according to *AARP The Magazine*:

1. Loveland/Fort Collins, Colorado
2. Bellingham, Washington
3. Raleigh/Durham/Chapel Hill, North Carolina
4. Sarasota, Florida
5. Fayetteville, Arkansas
6. Charleston, South Carolina
7. Asheville, North Carolina
8. San Diego, California
9. San Antonio, Texas
10. Santa Fe, New Mexico
11. Gainesville, Florida
12. Iowa City, Iowa
13. Portsmouth, New Hampshire

14. Spokane, Washington
15. Ashland, Oregon

By the way, the headline on the press release announcing the survey was surely written by a boomer: "*AARP The Magazine* Names the 15 Best Places to Reinvent Your Life."

State and Local Taxes

Information from sites like www.BestPlaces.net and www.Retire-mentLiving.com can give you a pretty good idea of state taxes around the country. But the wild card is property taxes, which are locally imposed and can vary widely within a state and even within a county. To get precise information, you will have to check the local tax rate for the town you're considering. You'll also need to check the assessment standards—that is, what percentage of a property's assessed valuation is taxed. This can be very important. One locality, for instance, may have a high rate but tax only a small percentage of assessed valuation; conversely, another locality may have a low rate but tax more of a home's assessed value, which could result in higher taxes than the first case.

The Tax Foundation, a nonprofit research organization in Washington, D.C., has a Web site (www.taxfoundation.org) that can help. Among other things, it lists the per-capita property taxes in the fifty states and the District of Columbia. Use the numbers with caution; they are only a rough guide because of the wide local variations in property taxes. Also, these are *per-capita* figures, which include the entire population of a state, not just property owners; individual property taxes are much higher than the per-capita amount. It is the *ranking* that can be a helpful guide.

Here's the Tax Foundation's list, ranked from highest to lowest according to the per-capita amount:

New Jersey ($1,519)
New Hampshire ($1,555)

Connecticut ($1,500)

New York ($1,329)

District of Columbia ($1,311)

Rhode Island ($1,233)

Vermont ($1,212)

Maine ($1,190)

Massachusetts ($1,084)

Illinois ($1,061)

Alaska ($1,046)

Wisconsin ($992)

Nebraska ($962)

Minnesota ($915)

Indiana ($869)

Texas ($852)

Iowa ($813)

Florida ($793)

Wyoming ($788)

Oregon ($787)

Kansas ($784)

Virginia ($780)

Colorado ($770)

Ohio ($745)

Pennsylvania ($732)

South Dakota ($729)

North Dakota ($721)

Maryland ($711)

Montana ($672)

Georgia ($662)

Michigan ($617)

California ($612)

Arizona ($607)

Idaho ($593)

Washington ($591)

Nevada ($573)

South Carolina ($553)

Utah ($537)

Missouri ($518)

North Carolina ($517)

Hawaii ($512)

Delaware ($467)

Mississippi ($454)

Tennessee ($436)

West Virginia ($420)

Oklahoma ($332)

Louisiana ($324)

Arkansas ($321)

Kentucky ($286)

New Mexico ($283)

Alabama ($210)

Www.RetirementLiving.com's Tom Wetzel says that because of the incredible variations in property taxes, it is extremely difficult to come to a definitive conclusion about which state is the least expensive. However, his Web site contains a ranking of states according to the total tax burden—expressed as a percentage of income—that each state imposes on its residents. The data come from the Census Bureau and include local property taxes, sales taxes, income taxes, and so on. They do not include any federal taxes, but they do take into account local and state taxes on businesses.

According to this list, the five states with the highest state and local tax burden are Maine, New York, Wisconsin, Hawaii, and Minnesota. The five lowest are Alaska, Tennessee, New Hampshire, Texas, and Alabama (tied with Colorado and South Dakota). If the District of Columbia were ranked with the states, it would actually be the highest, with its residents paying 13.9 percent of their income for local taxes. Here's the complete list of states, with the tax burden in each shown as a percentage of income:

Maine (12.8 percent)
New York (12.3 percent)
Wisconsin (12.0 percent)
Hawaii (11.6 percent)
Minnesota (11.3 percent)
Rhode Island (11.3 percent)
Arkansas (11.3 percent)
Utah (11.2 percent)
Ohio (11.2 percent)
Vermont (11.0 percent)
Connecticut (10.9 percent)
New Mexico (10.9 percent)
Nebraska (10.8 percent)
Michigan (10.7 percent)
Mississippi (10.7 percent)
Louisiana (10.5 percent)
Idaho (10.5 percent)
Kentucky (10.5 percent)
West Virginia (10.5 percent)
Washington (10.5 percent)
Kansas (10.4 percent)
Iowa (10.4 percent)
New Jersey (10.3 percent)
California (10.3 percent)
Georgia (10.2 percent)
North Dakota (10.2 percent)
Delaware (10.2 percent)
Arizona (10.1 percent)
North Carolina (10.1 percent)
South Carolina (10.0 percent)
Illinois (10.0 percent)
Montana (10.0 percent)
Oklahoma (9.9 percent)
Indiana (9.9 percent)

Pennsylvania (9.9 percent)

Wyoming (9.8 percent)

Maryland (9.7 percent)

Missouri (9.7 percent)

Massachusetts (9.5 percent)

Virginia (9.4 percent)

Oregon (9.4 percent)

Florida (9.3 percent)

Nevada (9.2 percent)

South Dakota (9.1 percent)

Colorado (9.1 percent)

Alabama (9.1 percent)

Texas (9.0 percent)

New Hampshire (8.6 percent)

Tennessee (8.4 percent)

Alaska (6.3 percent)

Though neither the per-capita ranking nor the income-linked ranking is perfect, the second list is probably more valuable for the average person than the per-capita list because of distortions from widely varying populations and incomes among the states. "This is the most realistic tax-burden charge I could find," Wetzel said. He pointed out that many traditionally low-tax states do not have the same level of services and education as do many higher-tax states. "But there are some very nice areas in these states," he said. "And if you don't have kids, the quality of schools may not be a factor. If you're just looking for a residence with not a lot of service— and you're not looking for a great appreciation on your property— then one of these states might be the place for you."

The RetirementLiving.com site provides roundups of the tax situation in each state. For instance, five states—Alaska, Delaware, Montana, New Hampshire, and Oregon—have no sales tax. Nine states have no personal income tax: Alaska, Florida, New Hampshire, Nevada, South Dakota, Tennessee, Texas, Washington, and

Wyoming. However, New Hampshire and Tennessee tax dividends and interest income that exceed certain limits. Florida has a small tax on the value of stocks and bonds held by individuals.

Of forty-one states that do have income taxes, twenty-six do not tax Social Security benefits. Some states have limited exemptions for different kinds of pensions.

Wetzel warns that sales taxes should be considered closely. Oklahoma, for instance, has a state sales tax of only 4.5 percent. But city and county governments together can increase that by up to 6.5 percentage points, which means the total sales tax could be as high as 11 percent, depending on where you live in the state. The same is true in Louisiana, where a state rate of 4 percent can reach 9.5 percent locally. "People need to look at the total tax picture as they try to shelter themselves as much as possible," Wetzel said. "Retirees may discover that some states are not the tax havens they are reported to be. A state may look inexpensive because it has no income tax, but it may have high property taxes or sales taxes. So the presence or absence of a state income tax may not be the best criterion for selecting a retirement destination. You also need to consider what tax relief is available for seniors."

While his site doesn't give specific information on local property taxes because they are so variable, it does give information on different statewide property tax breaks available to retirees. Wetzel stresses, however, that taxes and living costs are not the only factors you should consider in looking for a place to live. He cited ten considerations that he thought were important when surveying a town or area, but emphasized that the order of the list should be shuffled according to individual needs and tastes. Or, an item can be eliminated if it doesn't concern you. Here's his top ten list:

1. cost of living (including taxes)
2. climate
3. medical care

4. culture
5. distance from family and friends
6. crime
7. recreational opportunities
8. part-time employment opportunities
9. nearest airport
10. quality of restaurants

"A lot of people say they want to continue to work, at least part-time, in retirement, so they need to consider work opportunities," he said. "In a lot of rural areas, there are no Medicare HMO operations, and some physicians aren't taking new Medicare patients because the fees are being cut; perhaps you have a health problem that requires you to be near a good medical center. A retired music professor might move cultural opportunities higher on the list. Maybe you like to eat out a lot, or maybe you don't care about restaurants. How important is climate? All these things, not just taxes and living costs, need to be taken into consideration."

Don't Take My Word for It

When looking at comparative data on home prices around the country, be sure you understand the difference between average and median prices. You'll see both used, and they can provide sharply different pictures of the same situation. The average home price is the total value of a given number of homes divided by the number of homes. The median is the midpoint in a range of home prices: half fall above it, half fall below. It's good to look at the median, because the average can be skewed high by a few expensive homes. Of course, what you can't tell from the median alone is how far above and below the middle the range extends.

Bert Sperling of www.BestPlaces.net says a rule of thumb he follows is that the median price of homes is usually about 30 percent less than the average. Also keep in mind that data are going to vary—sometimes widely—depending on their sources. The best way to find out about home prices in an area in which you are interested is to go there and get a firsthand look and talk to local real estate agents.

It's also a good idea to take a short-term subscription to the local newspaper so you can study its real estate section. Most papers will sell three-month or six-month mail subscriptions. Many have Web sites providing access to much of their classified advertising, including real estate. It's still a good idea to get the printed paper because of photographs and display ads that may not be on a Web site. Also, getting the actual paper can help give you a better feeling for the community.

You can check out homes at www.Realtor.com, a Web site that allows you to search for a home by type (number of bedrooms and baths, for example) and price in cities and towns all over the country. Many of the listings have pictures and some have "virtual tours" that allow you to see panoramic views of various sections of a house, sometimes including a glimpse of its neighborhood.

Whenever I travel around the country I collect the little "real estate for sale" booklets you often see in roadside restaurants, malls, and real estate offices. Whether I look at home prices on the Internet, in newspapers, or in these booklets, I am constantly astounded at how low the prices are once you get out of the major metropolitan areas, particularly on the East Coast and West Coast. You can find an acceptable house for a lot less money. Period. Or, if you want to buy a house equal in value to the one you're moving from in a high-price area, you'll get a lot more for your money. A $400,000 home in Arkansas is going to be spectacular compared with a $400,000 house in San Francisco or New York.

I recently took a car trip through the eastern part of West Virginia just south of Hagerstown, Maryland, and on through the Blue Ridge Mountains of Virginia. It's a beautiful area of the country. As usual, I picked up several real estate booklets along the way. While there were certainly plenty of homes listed in the $200,000 to $300,000 price range, consider the following:

- A new home on a one-acre wooded lot. It has three bedrooms, two baths, vaulted ceilings, fully equipped kitchen, a fireplace, basement, and a deck with a hot tub. Asking price: $149,900.
- A two-story log home on five acres. It has three bedrooms and two baths. Price: $95,000.
- A ranch house on 1.77 acres. It has three bedrooms, two baths, a fireplace, deck, and a double garage. Price $119,000.

Of course, by the time this book is published, these houses will have been long sold and comparable houses may have risen a bit in price. These houses may not match your personal taste or be in an area in which you wish to live. But you get the idea.

By the way, if you're living in a cramped New York apartment that costs $300,000 a bedroom or in a $1 million four-room bungalow in California, there was a house for sale in West Virginia the likes of which might command your attention. It is a four-story brick and stone colonial with 7,000 square feet of space. Situated on 3.5 landscaped acres, it has six bedrooms, five full baths, and two half baths. It also has a finished basement and porches on two levels. The price: $580,000.

DRIVING DOWN STRESS

Jim and Kendra Golden made looking for a place to live a way of life, at least for a while. In the spring of 1999, the Goldens, both fifty-two at the time, left their jobs in New Jersey—he was an electrical engineer, she a lawyer—and took to the open road in a thirty-two-foot motor home. They had sold their house in Bergen County and were seeking a new place to live and a new life. They were looking for less stress and for new careers with rewards beyond money. Their son and daughter were both grown and on their own. "We were looking for a way to live more simply in jobs that are more rewarding, that bring value to society and ourselves," Kendra Golden said the following year in an interview for my "Seniority" column in the *New York Times*. "Our former jobs were mentally challenging, but we didn't always have a good sense when we went to bed at night that we were doing good for humanity or having a good life. For example, my job as a partner in a law firm involved a lot of foreclosure work. That was very stressful. Nobody's ever happy to see you coming."

Jim said he cherished the freedom of their nomadic life. "What has appealed to me has been not putting an automatic time limit on our travel, to just travel until it feels right to settle down," he said. "This has been a refreshing experience. My back and neck used to hurt from stress, but not any more." The Goldens even considered continuing their mobile life indefinitely, like the Hofmeisters in chapter 3.

After eighteen months of crisscrossing America—especially the West, to which they were particularly attracted—the Goldens settled in a small town on the Olympic Peninsula in Washington, northwest of Seattle. "The primary reason we stopped traveling was that we wanted to be part of a community again," Kendra said. They bought a house that cost less than half the price they had gotten for their former home in New Jersey. The new house, however, is much smaller. "This area is attracting a lot of people from California, so it's not the housing bargain that some parts of the country are," Jim said.

Although they were both raised in urban environments—he in the Atlanta area, she near Chicago—the two have adjusted well to small-town life. "We wanted off the fast track," Jim said. They especially like the scenic beauty of the area. They still have the motor home and use it for vacations, including a recent three-week trip through the Southwest.

Both are working, but in different careers. In New Jersey, Jim worked mainly in the sales and management areas of electrical engineering. He now works as a computer consultant for a non-profit concern that provides long-term employment for people with disabilities. Kendra, who says she has no plans to ever again practice law, works for a nonprofit center for arts and education.

"Our life has radically changed," Jim said. "We make substantially less money. But we have a very rich life without a lot of money. Back east, the automatic thing was to go out to an expensive place for dinner. Here, we are less likely to do that. We might go to someone's house for a meal, or just take a hike together."

"We are very happy," Kendra added. "We love being in a small town as opposed to a suburban metropolitan area."

Her husband added: "Never say never, but I don't ever see us coming back to a big urban community. I'm busier than I've ever been before. Sometimes I miss the freedom of our life on the road. But we know we can always go back on the road again if our life doesn't have the same appeal in a few years."

Kendra agreed. "I can see us hitting the road again in the motor home more than I can see us returning to our previous lives," she said.

Key No. 1: Your Assets

We have no children. I want to spend my last dime with my last breath.
—ALECK TOWNSLEY

For most people, their most important asset is the equity in their homes. This is especially true for those who have owned a house for ten years or more in high-cost urban areas. The appreciation in real estate prices in these sections of the country has been staggering. Even if price increases slow—or even if home values decline some-what—these homeowners are sitting on assets that could unlock the door to early retirement. Their homes are piggy banks containing money they deposited over the years as they paid their mortgages, as well as money from the appreciated value of their property.

MORE THAN A PLACE TO LIVE

The Office of Federal Housing Enterprise Oversight (OFHEO), a government agency that tracks changes in home values, has a Web site (www.ofheo.gov) with all kinds of data on home prices around the United States. For instance, average home values across the United States increased by 181.6 percent from 1980 through

September 30, 2002. For the most recent five years, the gain was 38.6 percent, and for the year it was 6.2 percent—in both cases through September 30, 2002.

However, for those living in New England, the Middle Atlantic states, or the Pacific Coast area, the average increases were much higher. For New England, the gain since 1980 was 347.7 percent, with the five-year period and most recent year coming in at 62 percent and 9.8 percent, respectively. For the Middle Atlantic region, it was 251.6 percent, 43.1 percent, and 9.2 percent. The Pacific Coast was 237.8 percent, 52.2 percent, and 7.6 percent.

Remember that these gains are averages. There are some areas within these regions that had much bigger gains, some much smaller. The difference in home values, as well as price gains, within even a relatively small area can be dramatic. For instance, according to www.BestPlaces.net, the median (half are above, half are below— more about median and average later in this chapter) home value in Scottsdale, Arizona, is $195,620. Yet in 2003, the *Wall Street Journal* listed median values for homes in Scottsdale of $405,000, $496,000, and $428,000. Why the big difference? Well, there are twenty zip codes in Scottsdale, and the newspaper had selected the median values of homes in three of the most expensive, 85259, 85255, and 85262. Www.BestPlaces.net's figure took all the zip codes into account. The same kinds of gaps can occur for increases in home values, depending on locations even within specific towns.

Housing Across the United States

OFHEO uses nine regional divisions created by the U.S. Census Bureau (see figure 3).

Figure 4 shows the agency's ranking of the nine regions.

The agency's Web site offers a lot more information on home prices, including the ranking of 185 so-called metropolitan statistic areas, or MSAs, based on increases in home values over various time periods. There's also a state-by-state ranking for various time periods, including from 1980 through September 30, 2002.

Figure 3

U.S. Census Divisions

Pacific
Alaska, Hawaii, Washington, Oregon, California

West North Central
North Dakota, South Dakota, Minnesota, Nebraska, Iowa, Kansas, Missouri

East North Central
Michigan, Wisconsin, Illinois, Indiana, Ohio

New England
Maine, New Hampshire, Vermont, Massachusetts, Connecticut, Rhode Island

Middle Atlantic
New York, New Jersey, Pennsylvania

South Atlantic
Maryland, Delaware, West Virginia, Virginia, North Carolina, South Carolina, Georgia, Florida

Mountain
Idaho, Montana, Wyoming, Nevada, Utah, Colorado, Arizona, New Mexico

West South Central
Oklahoma, Arkansas, Texas, Louisiana

East South Central
Kentucky, Tennessee, Mississippi, Alabama

All these statistics for home values around the country are interesting, but in the end they are just numbers. The number that really counts is the amount you sell your home for minus a real estate agent's fee and whatever you owe on the mortgage: the dollars you can walk away with.

The point is to have this walk-away amount be enough for you to buy another home free and clear—or mostly so—in a less expensive area, like the Taaffe family in chapter 4. Or, if you are at least sixty-two and want to stay put, you can take out a reverse mortgage on your home. Whichever path you elect, you are using your home to make your retirement work. Remember, it's your money locked up in that house. Use it to achieve your goals.

Figure 4

Changes in House Prices Around the Country

In recent years, real estate has risen in value much more rapidly, on average, in some regions of the country than in others. The regions in the chart are the Census Bureau divisions shown in figure 3. The data is for time periods ended September 30, 2002.

Region	*Change in the most recent...*			Change since 1980	Rank
	Quarter	Year	Five years		
New England	+1.4%	+9.8%	+62.0%	+347.7%	1
Middle Atlantic	+1.3	+9.2	+43.1	+251.6	2
Pacific	+1.6	+7.6	+52.2	+237.8	3
National average	+0.8	+6.2	+38.6	+181.6	
South Atlantic	+1.0	+6.7	+36.5	+170.7	4
East North Central	0.0	+3.7	+28.9	+166.4	5
Mountain	+0.6	+3.7	+31.7	+156.1	6
West North Central	+0.1	+5.1	+37.8	+144.8	7
East South Central	+0.7	+3.1	+23.6	+133.2	8
West South Central	+0.2	+3.1	+28.6	+80.9	9

Source: Office of Federal Housing Enterprise Oversight

To Renovate or Not

I am often puzzled when I hear people who are planning to sell their homes talking about first remodeling or making some fairly major repairs—like giving the kitchen a makeover or adding a bathroom. You often hear comments like, "Well, you know, if you put in another bathroom, you'll get 90 percent of the cost back when you sell the house." Think about that. If I suggested you give me $10,000 and then in a few months or a year I would give you back $9,000, you'd think I was crazy. But that's exactly what you're doing if you add a $10,000 bathroom to a house you plan to sell soon and get back 90 percent of the cost.

Even if you were to get back 100 percent, what's the point? That would be like investing the $10,000 at zero interest. Some improvements might make a house sell faster ("curb appeal," some real estate agents call it) or make it appeal to a broader group of buyers. But it is going to cost you money, all of which you may not get back.

However, doing work on a house that you plan to live in for, say five to ten years, might make sense. In that case, you'd be getting the use of and pleasure from the improvements, plus the appreciation of the house over the years might well allow you to recoup the repair costs, or even more.

Another mistake is to overimprove a house beyond what is normal for a neighborhood. It could be very difficult to sell the house for enough money to get back even a high percentage of your costs. Houses on my street sell within a price range that does not vary all that much—no matter what improvements have been made.

To build or improve beyond the neighborhood norm might be more reasonable if you plan to stay in your house forever. Then you don't have to be concerned about getting your money back. I have friends who have turned their Victorian home into a showplace far beyond most houses in their area. They have used the best and most expensive materials, including custom-made components. They have no plans to sell their house, however, and expect to enjoy it for the rest of their lives. That makes sense from a personal satisfaction point of view.

But if you're planning to sell your house relatively soon, think hard about putting money into improvements A new roof or a new paint job may move the house faster, but is it worth it? You also run the risk of selecting a color that may not appeal to some buyers. Maybe it would be better to take a few weeks longer to sell the house as it is. Or drop the asking price a bit and explain that this is to allow the buyer to do his or her own painting or reroofing.

There are exceptions. Your house, for instance, has to be in working order. It would be tough to sell a home with a broken heating system. If your wall-to-wall carpets are worn and dirty— and they are covering hardwood floors—it might pay to spend $1,000 to $2,000 to take up the carpets and refinish the floors. An improvement like that might pay for itself and then some.

Seek the advice of an independent home appraiser on such

matters. Also, there are many organizations and publications that have lists showing what percentage of a home remodeling or repair investment you can expect to get back when you sell your house. A good place to check for such information is *Smart Money* magazine's Web site (www.smartmoney.com).

Be aware, though, that these payback estimates are all over the place and even vary within a given city or region. Many of the lists estimate that you will get back 90 to 100 percent for things like adding a bathroom, remodeling a kitchen, or adding a new heating system. On the other hand, you're likely to get back only 15 to 60 percent for finishing a basement, adding a swimming pool, or upgrading the landscaping.

So if you're planning to sell your house and retire, be very careful about spending money for repairs that you may not get back. Remember: cutting expenses increases income.

REVERSE MORTGAGES: A THIRD WAY

A surprising number of people have never heard of reverse mortgages or have only the vaguest idea about them.

AARP points out on its excellent reverse mortgage Web site (www.aarp.org/revmort) that until the beginning of federally insured reverse mortgages in 1989, there were only two main ways to get cash—an owner's equity—out of a house. You could sell it, but then you would have to move. Or you could borrow against the value of your home, but that meant monthly payments to repay the loans. And if for some reason you couldn't make those monthly payments, you would risk losing your house—the collateral for the loan.

AARP was one of the prime forces in getting federal legislation passed to insure reverse mortgages—thus allowing what the group calls "a third way" of getting money from your home without leaving it or facing monthly payments.

The concept of a reverse mortgage, or home-equity conversion, is simple: you borrow against your home's value, but you are not required to make any repayments of principal or interest as long as you stay put. The amount you owe will grow larger—and your equity will shrink—as time goes by because you are making no payments. It's the reverse of a conventional mortgage in which your debt declines and your equity rises as you make payments. If you move or die with a reverse mortgage, you or your heirs must pay back the loan, including interest and charges, usually by selling the house. In the meantime, no one can kick you out as long as your pay your property taxes and homeowners insurance and maintain the house.

Here's a really good part: if you live long enough for the accumulating interest to push the total debt above your home's value, the difference is paid by insurance that is built into the loan. That means the mortgage company can't touch anything else in your estate. This is known as a nonrecourse loan. In other words, a lender's only recourse for getting the loan repaid is the value of the home in question.

You can receive the proceeds, which are generally not subject to taxes, from a reverse mortgage in several ways:

- As a credit line (except in Texas), with either a fixed limit or a limit whose balance will increase each year equal to the interest rate you are charged.
- In a lump-sum cash payment.
- In monthly payments for a specified number of years or as long as you live in your home.

You're not stuck with one choice. The payment options can be blended or even changed later.

If you take the lump-sum cash payment, you could invest the proceeds in an annuity that would provide monthly payments to you for the rest of your life, no matter where you live.

Martha York, a widow in Port St. Lucie, Florida, needed to

supplement her monthly income of about $1,200 from Social Security and an annuity. In 1998, when she was seventy-five she took out a reverse mortgage on her home, then valued at $80,000. She elected to take a combination of a $5,000 lump-sum payment and $300 a month for life. This boosted her monthly income by 25 percent, to $1,500. She has been pleased with her decision, which also allowed her to make some improvements to her home. "It's a terrific thing," she said. "I intend to live long enough to use up all the value in my house and then some."

In January 2003, Peter and Ruth Ricca of Metairie, Louisiana, took out a reverse mortgage on their home to, as Ruth Ricca put it, "give us a pad, an extra bit of money to make us feel comfortable." She was seventy-eight; he was eighty. The two had retired from the grocery and restaurant business more than a decade and a half earlier as they had each turned sixty-two. They had only their Social Security benefits and savings to live on. When they applied for the reverse mortgage, their house was valued at $230,000. They elected to take a lump-sum payment of $105,000. They used $15,000 of that to pay off a bank loan and used another $15,000 to pay some additional bills. The remaining $75,000 they put away to be used as necessary. "We're very happy with the arrangement," Ruth said.

Help from HUD

While the concept behind reverse mortgages is simple, they have many variations and the details are complex. Over the years, this has led some borrowers to turn unnecessarily to outside agents, who have charged fees of up to 10 percent of a loan for "referral" services and information that is available free from the government and other sources.

That's one reason the Department of Housing and Urban Development, the primary insurer of reverse mortgages, requires consumers to confer with HUD-approved counselors before getting these federally insured loans. The only fees you should ever pay are regular loan application and origination fees—directly to the lender. These fees do not have to be paid up front. They can become a part of the loan.

To qualify, homeowners must be sixty-two. Obviously, you must have equity in your home, but it does not have to be fully paid for. There are no income requirements. Mobile homes are not eligible, although modular and manufactured homes are okay if they are permanent and taxed as real estate, not motor vehicles.

Condominiums are also eligible for the federally insured loans, although cooperative apartments are not. Ken Scholen, a reverse mortgage specialist with AARP, says HUD is moving to make co-ops eligible. The difficulty with co-ops is that owners do not own their homes directly, but instead own shares in an entity that owns their property. One lender, Financial Freedom in Irvine, California, has a pilot program for co-op reverse mortgages in New York City. Because they are not federally insured, these mortgages cost a bit more, but they are still nonrecourse loans and all the other rules and safeguards apply.

The interest rates charged for federally insured reverse mortgages are adjustable and based on the one-year Treasury rate. "Generally, annually adjustable reverse mortgage rates will be a bit less than rates for an annually adjustable forward, or conventional, mortgage," Scholen said. Federally insured reverse mortgages— under a program called Home Equity Conversion Mortgage, or HECM—are by far the most popular, accounting for more than 90 percent of all such loans.

Is It for You?

The amount you can borrow through a federally insured reverse mortgage is limited, regardless of your home's value, and varies from state to state and even from county to county. The AARP reverse mortgage Web site has a calculator that will tell you how much you can borrow based on your home's value, your age, and where you live. If you owe money on your home, generally you must pay it off before you get a reverse mortgage, or pay off the loan with the money you get from the reverse mortgage. The older you are, the more you can borrow. At the Web site you can also download, order online, or order by telephone a free AARP book titled *Home Made Money: A Consumer's Guide to Reverse Mortgages.*

Keep in mind that even though you can have a reverse mortgage and live in your house as long as you want, the loan must be paid off when you move or die. If you want to leave your home free and clear to your children, then a reverse mortgage may not be for you. Also, because of the loan fees and charges, a reverse mortgage is more expensive in the early years of the loan. Therefore, it's a bad idea to take out a reverse mortgage if you plan to sell your house anytime soon.

You don't have to be pressed for cash to get a reverse mortgage. Aleck and Sheila Townsley are comfortable retired in Foster City, California, in a house that overlooks San Francisco Bay. They are able to live well on retirement incomes from his career as a lawyer and her years as a teacher. But in 1999, when they were both sixty-five, they used their home—then valued at $555,000— for a reverse mortgage. They chose a $65,000 line of credit that would eventually grow to $170,000 so they could afford "extras" like travel. "We have no children," Aleck Townsley said. "I want to spend my last dime with my last breath."

The advantages of a reverse mortgage are clear if you want to stay in your current home when you retire. Such a loan can also be helpful even if you plan to sell your home and use the equity to pay cash for another house in a less expensive area. In the hypothetical case of Joe and Sue Sample in chapter 2, they could sell their house in the New York area and be able to pay cash for a home in Tucson, Arizona. When they are old enough to qualify, they could easily take out a reverse mortgage on the Arizona home. In one sense, they would be getting the best of both worlds since the proceeds from a reverse mortgage represent only a portion of the equity in a home. The Samples would get all their equity, $189,000, out of their East Coast house. The Tucson home might cost $120,000 and they would be able to use another $39,000 to pay off debts and relocate. The remaining $30,000 would be added to their savings. A reverse mortgage on the new home would be gravy on top of the equity realized from the first house.

If you are sixty-two and find yourself house rich and cash poor, a reverse mortgage could be an important part of your retirement plans.

In September 2002, Kathleen Maddox, a widow in Billings, Montana, turned sixty-two. That same month she applied for a reverse mortgage. "I did it right away, as soon as I was sixty-two and eligible," she said. "I was pretty low on money." Her husband had died ten years earlier and she had been a homemaker most of her life except for part-time work in the schools her four children attended.

Her home was valued at $118,000, and she selected a reverse mortgage that provided her with a $41,000 line of credit. The balance in her line of credit will grow each year at a rate equal to the interest she is being charged for the reverse mortgage. Maddox planned to use some of the money for repairs on her house, and was considering buying a used, but newer, car. She is also doing some traveling for her "mental health." She is the sole caregiver for a ninety-two-year-old mother. "It was time for me to have a break," she said. The Thanksgiving after she got the loan, Maddox went to Phoenix to visit a sister for two weeks. Then at Christmas she visited another sister in North Dakota. She was also contemplating trips to Canada and Alaska, where she has friends. She is pleased with how things have worked out. Her grown children—a daughter in Seattle and three sons in the Billings area—had no objections when she decided on a reverse mortgage. "They told me, 'If that's what you want to do, Mom, go for it,' " she said.

THE MILLIONAIRE IN THE ROOM

Before we consider assets other than your home, let's look at some figures on the net worth of Americans provided by the Federal Reserve Board. They will help to explain how misleading it can be to look only at averages rather than considering the median as well.

As illustrated by what seemed to be a discrepancy between estimates of home prices in Scottsdale, Arizona, by www.Best Places.net and the *Wall Street Journal*, you need to look very carefully at what figures represent and how they were calculated.

For example, if there are five people in a room making annual salaries of $10,000, $15,000, $20,000, $30,000, and $40,000, the average salary is $23,000; the median is $20,000. Nobody in the room makes the average salary, but it is not greatly unrepresentative of the group. Now assume someone making $1 million a year enters the room. Suddenly the average salary jumps to $185,833.33 a year. That "average" is very misleading and is not representative of any of the salaries in the room. The addition of the millionaire raises the median to only $25,000. So you have a better picture if you know the median and compare it with the average; you can see that there's a lopsided number, or value, that is driving the average up or down.

Wherever possible—this is especially true for home values— look at median figures as well as averages. There's a good Web site (www.mathsisfun.com) on these and other data and math calculations.

Every three years the Fed releases data on family net worth, which the agency defines as "the difference between families' gross assets and their liabilities." The most recent figures available are for 2001.

The effects of the bull market and roaring economy of the 1990s are evident when 2001 data are compared with data from 1998 and 1992. Median wealth rose 10.4 percent from 1998 to 2001 and

40.5 percent from 1992 to 2001. The mean, or average, rose 28.7 percent in the shorter period and 71.6 percent in the longer span.

For 2001, the median net worth of all families was $86,100; the average was $395,500. What does this lopsided median-average ratio tell us? There are some millionaires—and billionaires—in the room driving the average up, that's what. Income distribution in the United States is skewed toward the top, a trend that has been accelerating in recent years.

For families with a head of household who is fifty-five to sixty-four years old, the median net worth was $181,500; the average was $727,000.

The Fed then used stock index data that measured the drop in the value of equities between October 4, 2001, and October 4, 2002, to adjust the net worth for all families to account for the effects of the swooning market. This calculation reduced the median net worth of all families by 6.3 percent, to $80,700, and the average net worth by 13.7 percent, to $341,000.

CONSIDER ALL YOUR ASSETS

Chapter 8 contains a worksheet for calculating your net worth: basically adding up your assets (what you own) and liabilities (what you owe) and subtracting the latter from the former. There's also a handy consumer Web site (www.practicalmoneyskills.com) that can help with this and much more.

Your retirement plans may well include turning some noncash assets into money. This means selling things you don't need: those extra cars or some furniture that may not fit in a smaller house. If you can't get a fair price, donate the items to charity and take a tax deduction. First, of course, check with the Internal Revenue Service or a tax adviser for the rules on such deductions.

Depending on where you live, it might be a smart idea to hold a yard sale. This can be a great way to clear out a lot of things you might not want to carry into the next, less expensive, phase of your life. Depending on what you're selling, you might be surprised at the money you take in. In the early 1980s, my wife and I were moving from a house in Houston to a small apartment in New York City. We held a Saturday yard sale. We advertised in the classifieds and put up posters in the neighborhood and notices on bulletin boards in local grocery stores, health clubs, and community centers. The sale was scheduled to start at 9 A.M., but at 6 we had antique and used furniture dealers ringing our doorbell. They wanted to see what we had before it was picked over. The day was sunny and mild, and we had a steady stream of buyers. Our total take was a bit over $3,000.

Because we weren't thinking much about retirement in those days, we spent the money. But had we invested it at 6.5 percent, it would have grown to more than $10,000 by now. If we had invested it at 6.5 percent and added just $100 a month, it would now be worth almost $60,000. Had we put it in a mutual fund that took advantage of the stock boom of the 1990s—let's assume 12 percent growth—and added the same $100 a month, that $3,000 would today be worth more than $120,000.

I don't even remember how we spent the $3,000. Talk about missed opportunities!

Don't Overlook Social Security

When you're trying to balance your assets and liabilities against your needs when you retire, don't forget Social Security—or sell it short. Although chapter 7 looks at Social Security in greater detail, I think it's important to view it as an asset that you will have access to when you are sixty-two. The longer you wait to collect it, the more you get. But, presumably, if you are trying to figure out how to retire early you are likely to tap into your Social Security benefits as soon as possible.

Again, consider Joe and Sue Sample. Their combined Social Security benefits when they are sixty-two will be $26,400 a year for as long as they live. Assume for a moment that the $26,400 represents the 4 percent that a retiree can withdraw from a nest egg without depleting it. Looking at it that way, the $26,400 payout represents savings of more than $650,000. Now that's not the way Social Security works. But $650,000 does represent the amount you would need to replace the Social Security benefit of $26,400 so that the payment would not run out in your lifetime. Remember, too, that Social Security benefits increase along with the cost of living, so that theoretical "savings" of $650,000 also increases accordingly.

I know some financial planners and accountants would probably cringe at this approach because of the pay-as-you-go structure of Social Security. But you have contributed to Social Security all your working life and are entitled to the benefits. Why not view them as an asset like anything else?

"Follow Your Bliss"

Another "asset" you should consider is yourself. Survey after survey shows that most people, especially the baby boomers, do not want a traditional retirement that is akin to being constantly on vacation. People want to be challenged and stimulated in this next phase of life, and that will often include working. It doesn't mean a traditional job, or even a part-time job, and all the baggage that goes with it. After all, you are planning early retirement to free yourself from wage slavery. You don't want to jump from the frying pan into the fire!

"Follow your bliss," admonished the late teacher and scholar Joseph Campbell. That's pretty good advice, especially as you contemplate your second act. What is your bliss or your passion or your interest? What turns you on? Is there a hobby you really like? Many times there is little relationship between what you do for a living and your bliss. Think of those stories you read in newspapers of grandfathers and grandmothers who have returned to college to finish their degrees or go to medical school. They are following their bliss. Grandma Moses, a farm wife, was in her seventies when she taught herself to paint. "If I didn't start painting, I would have raised chickens," she told Edward R. Murrow in a television interview. "I would never sit back in a rocking chair, waiting for someone to help."

If you're uncertain about your bliss, you probably need to embark on some self-exploration and discovery to find what you really enjoy doing and what makes you happy. Try some new things. Ever think you might like to teach? There's a teacher shortage in many parts of the country, and for those with a college degree it's not hard to get a teaching certificate in most states.

Sometimes the connection takes a little creativity, but often your bliss can be an income-producing asset.

I knew an electrical engineer who was an avid bicycle rider. Just before he retired, he spent three weeks at a school for bicycle mechanics. After he retired, he took a part-time job working as a repairman in a bicycle shop and also organizing local bicycle tours; he later opened his own repair shop. He's making money and following his bliss.

A French orthopedic surgeon with a lifelong passion for art retired and applied for admission to a prestigious art academy. He was accepted and today his paintings sell briskly.

Then there's a retired English professor who became a broker in Navajo rugs after years of collecting them as a hobby.

The possibilities are truly endless and limited only by your imagination and interests. It is usually true that if you are where you want to be and doing what you want to do, things have an uncanny way of falling into place. Joseph Campbell added that if you follow your bliss, "doors will open where you would not have thought there would be doors, and where there wouldn't be a door for anyone else." He also wrote that following your bliss puts you "on a kind of track, which has been there all the while waiting for you, and the life that you ought to be living is the one you are living."

Retirement can give you the opportunity to restore harmony to your life if you follow Campbell's advice. Better, of course, to have followed it from the beginning. But we are not perfect. Retirement gives us a second chance.

Class Starts When the Phone Rings

The historian David McCullough has said that most people have in their homes one of the most amazing research and learning devices ever invented: the lowly telephone. If you don't know something, he says, call someone who does. Alexander Graham Bell's invention has some other virtues that McCullough didn't mention. It is wonderfully interactive, binding us together over great distances. It is very reliable. And it doesn't have to be upgraded every six months.

The value of the telephone is not lost on Dorot, a nonprofit social services organization for the elderly in New York City that runs, among other activities, an educational program called University Without Walls. Through telephone conference calls, it takes courses and support-group sessions to older people and those with limited mobility. "Some people say University Without Walls is their life," said Bonnie Jacobs, director of educational services at Dorot. "They're either on the phone taking courses or talking to people they met through the courses." The program allows Dorot (Hebrew for "generations") to reach beyond its base in the New York metropolitan area. Some of its eight hundred students, who range in age from forty to one hundred, live in Florida, Maryland, Utah, and Israel. One teacher conducts his classes from his home in Switzerland, another from Arizona. Information is available on Dorot's Web site, www.dorotusa.org; prospective students can register by calling Dorot in Manhattan at (212) 769-2850 or toll-free at (877) 819-9147.

Dorot offers a variety of noncredit courses covering literature, history, science, and the arts, along with how-to classes and support-group sessions for particular problems, like dealing with Medicare or certain health or psychological difficulties. Many classes, fifty minutes each, run once a week for a full fourteen-week semester.

Others last a few weeks, and some are single sessions. The registration fee is $10 a semester, plus a $10 charge for each course. There is no charge for single-session classes, and Dorot waives fees for those who have difficulty paying. It also pays all phone charges. Classes may have just five students or as many as eighteen.

To participate, all a student has to do is be at the phone at the appointed time. When it rings, a staff member from the Dorot office on the Upper West Side of New York is on the line to link him or her to a conference call and to take roll. Then the teacher, or "facilitator," takes over. After fifty minutes, the staff member breaks in and announces that the class is over. For some courses, printed material is sent out in advance.

I recently participated in a class titled "The Glamour Gals and Guys of the '30s and '40s," taught by Bill Hubschmitt, sixty-seven, a movie buff and semiretired accountant who lives in Sedona, Arizona. Clair, Sarah, Sally, Gilda, Pat, Linda, Eleanor, Evelyn, and Larry all responded to roll call before the class was turned over to Hubschmitt. The next fifty minutes were a trip back in time through a captivating, well-organized, and relatively in-depth discussion of the singers Alice Fay and Jane Powell, as well as an introduction to Judy Garland, a subject that would be carried over to the next week's class. The students were encouraged to chime in and express their opinions. Some did, but the presence of a stranger, and a journalist at that, might have inhibited the others.

Hubschmitt, who has been teaching at Dorot for six years, said he thought his course was especially good for older students. "It's nostalgic for them and involves a lot of memory recall," he said. "Often they'll express an opinion about whether they liked or disliked a star. We agree to disagree. I think it helps to stimulate their minds."

After living and working in New York for sixty years, Hubschmitt moved to Arizona three and a half years ago. He is a lifelong student of film and has more than three hundred silent films in his video collection. "I grew up in New York City in a large family," he said. "The only entertainment, the only escape from tenement life, was the movies, which I started going to when I was five or six."

Bonnie Jacobs, the director, says many people who take the course make friends with others in the class. "We encourage this," she said. "Sometimes they'll even create study groups outside of class."

Myrna Shapiro, sixty-seven, is a retired professor who divides her time between West Palm Beach, Florida, and Jericho, New York. She has been a University Without Walls student for seven years. She takes ten to twelve classes a semester. "I was a science major," she said, "and I especially enjoy the liberal arts courses." She added, "This program is a godsend for people with vision problems."

Zelda Hearst, seventy-five, a retired widow in Sunnyside, Queens, was a student and now teaches several courses, including self-help ones like "Things I'm Afraid Of," "You're Getting on My Nerves," and "Mother-in-Law: Enemy or Ally." She has made many telephone friends since she began teaching in 1994, including Myrna Shapiro, whom she has never met in person. "Sometimes the anonymity of phone friends is good and a special thing," she said. "It's like having an e-mail friend, only you can hear the person's voice, which I prefer. It's human contact. E-mail doesn't do much for me."

6

Key No. 2: Health Insurance

Life is so much better for millions of Americans because of Medicare.
—ROBERT M. HAYES, PRESIDENT, MEDICARE RIGHTS CENTER

If this were Canada or Europe or almost any other modern industrialized country, you wouldn't be reading this chapter. That's because the United States is one of the few nations that doesn't offer some form of national health insurance regardless of where you work, or whether you work at all. Such coverage in this country—Medicare—is offered only to those sixty-five or older. If you want to retire before you are sixty-five, you're on your own for health insurance.

Some people are lucky. They work for companies that provide health benefits to retirees. But this is a shrinking benefit. Fewer than a third of companies now offer it, according to a survey by William M. Mercer, a benefits consulting company. In 1993, almost half did. This is a big problem for many people in their mid-fifties and early sixties. You don't have to spend much time talking to people in that age group in today's high-stress workforce to learn that the urge to retire is pervasive. Many want an early exit, but not without health insurance. They rightly fear that one serious illness could wipe them out financially.

Most people planning early retirement can figure out ways to pay for health insurance, although it can be a burden. They can never budget for—or realistically hope to pay by themselves—the uninsured costs of a serious accident or catastrophic illness. However, as we will see later in this chapter, the situation is not as daunting as it seems. There are some options; with a little care it is possible to build a health care bridge that will carry you from early retirement to Medicare.

Once eligible for Medicare, many people—unless they are enrolled in a Medicare health maintenance organization—buy private supplemental Medigap insurance to broaden their coverage.

HEALTH INSURANCE: NOT OUR FINEST HOUR

Health insurance in this country is in a shambles. There are at least 41 million people without coverage, according to the Census Bureau. This number swells to 75 million when it includes those who were without health insurance at some point in the two years up to March 2003, according to Families USA, a consumer advocacy group in Washington.

People without insurance are not just the poor and unemployed. According to the Census Bureau, 17.7 percent of them have household incomes between $25,000 and $49,999, while 11.3 percent have household incomes between $50,000 and $74,999; another 7.7 percent make more than $75,000 a year. The census figures also show that 13.1 percent of all those between forty-five and sixty-five years of age have no health insurance.

According to the Employee Benefit Research Institute, there are approximately 25.9 million Americans in the fifty-five-to-sixty-four age group. A total of 4.3 million of them, or about one-sixth, are retired. Of those retirees, 55.8 percent have coverage through their former employers, 12.2 percent buy individual policies, and 17.8 percent have no health insurance. The remainder fall into other categories: coverage under Medicaid, for example, or under Medicare because they are disabled.

The Solution That Won't Take

I believe that the only realistic long-term answer to the health insurance crisis in America is some form of universal health care. However, we don't have such a system right now, so if you'd like to go directly to the practical side of health insurance, skip ahead to the section entitled "When You Have to Buy Health Insurance."

There have been moves over the years to bring universal health coverage to America, but all have met failure. The most recent major effort was President Bill Clinton's proposal in the early 1990s. There have also been failed efforts to extend Medicare to everyone.

One of the most interesting proposals for a type of universal coverage was made in 1972 by the late senator Russell B. Long, a Louisiana Democrat. It was called federal catastrophic health insurance and enjoyed a degree of bipartisan support, although Congress never passed it. It may have been ahead of its time. Senator Long's plan would have had the government pay all medical costs above an annual deductible of $2,000 for those not covered by Medicare. (Today, of course, that deductible might be more like $8,000 to $10,000.) Insurance companies would have underwritten much of the government's coverage. In addition, they could have sold private policies covering the deductible portion. For people who couldn't afford the deductible or insurance for it, Medicaid would have paid.

It's difficult to find much wrong with this plan and it would certainly have been a boon to people who want to retire but are too young for Medicare. The proposal would have included participation by private insurance companies and would have covered everyone. People who did not qualify for Medicaid could have paid the deductible themselves, bought insurance for it, or had coverage provided by their employers. Because insurance companies' exposure for the deductible would have been limited to paying a relatively small, capped amount each year, such policies would have been much less expensive than conventional ones. Because costs would be low, small businesses would have been encouraged to offer deductible coverage to their workers.

Catastrophic insurance would for the most part avoid the bureaucracy that many people fear with national health insurance, because most Americans would be unlikely ever to use it. For people over sixty-five, who usually have the biggest medical expenses, coverage would be provided by Medicare.

Jay Constantine, who worked for the Senate Finance Committee in the 1970s when Senator Long was chairman, said that there was nothing wrong with the plan then—or now. "It empowers people," he said. "It gives them health care separate from corporations or their employers. This is especially important in the kind of mobile society we have now. It is the right track and the least costly approach to getting everybody covered."

James J. Mongan, who was also on the staff of the Senate committee and later served as president of Massachusetts General Hospital in Boston, called catastrophic insurance a "good plan for the middle class." He said Senator Long was "ahead of his time."

Alice M. Rivlin, a senior fellow at the Brookings Institution who is a former Federal Reserve governor and former director of the Office of Management and Budget, thinks such a catastrophic insurance plan ought to be revived. "It's viable and worth considering again," she said. Both she and Constantine said that such a plan could hold down costs, especially among those who pay the deductible themselves.

While such a plan would certainly fit the needs of many early retirees, Rivlin wondered how popular it would be with the general population. "Americans are a bit irrational about health care," she said. "They like first-dollar coverage; they like to have all their health care covered rather than thinking of insurance as protection against large expenditures, which is what catastrophic is."

The Medicare Scare

The fears that many people, especially conservatives, have about government involvement in national health care is also a bit irrational.

Henry J. Aaron, a senior fellow at the Brookings Institution and an authority on health care financing, points out that when the law creating Medicare was passed in 1965, the American Medical Association called it "a deception and a danger that would threaten the relationship between patients and doctors." He recalled that "the head of the AMA even likened his group's fight against Medicare to Winston Churchill's stand against the Nazis." Aaron added, "Ronald Reagan, then a politically active movie actor, said that Medicare was symptomatic of socialism that would 'invade every area of freedom in this country' and force Americans to spend their 'sunset years telling our children and our children's children what it was like in America when men were free.'"

Medicare, of course, went on to become one of the great success stories of the twentieth century and has proved immensely popular with the public. "Life is so much better for millions of Americans because of Medicare," said Robert M. Hayes, the president of the Medicare Rights Center, which helps individuals deal with Medicare-related problems.

Medicare has not just improved the lot of older Americans. It has also empowered younger people who no longer have to worry about their parents' medical bills. Prior to 1965, younger people were faced with the real possibility that caring for a sick parent, retired and no longer covered by health insurance, could strap them financially. In too many cases, it did.

Because Medicare frees you from having to worry about your parents' medical bills, it may also allow you to retire early even though you may not be eligible for its coverage.

It Works in Canada

Still, the chance of a Medicare-like program—universal health care—for all Americans is dim. So too is the possibility of a catastrophic health plan like the one proposed by Senator Long in the 1970s. Conservatives' strong dislike of government involvement and increasingly powerful lobbying by big drug and insurance companies are formidable barriers. Drug companies fear price controls and a pinch on profits; insurance companies don't want the government horning in on their business.

In many ways, that's unfortunate. Some form of national health insurance that is not linked to where we work would certainly be more appropriate for modern America's mobile, job-hopping population. The old social contracts and bonds that once existed between companies and their workers are mostly history, but the health insurance tie remains. The result is that many people, especially as they get older, are forced to work just to maintain health coverage. The situation is a stranglehold on the dreams and aspirations of a lot of people.

In Canada and most European countries, this is not an issue. Even the most conservative politicians in these nations usually support universal health care for their citizens.

American criticisms of national health programs are sometimes based on groundless fears or simply incorrect information. I remember a conservative radio talk-show host several years ago who claimed that there were only two CT-scan machines for all of Canada! Someone finally got through on his call-in line to correct him, but for listeners who had switched stations or turned off the radio the damage had been done.

This same radio host later told stories he had heard about Canadians who were flocking to the United States for medical care, fleeing their own country's "socialized medicine." A few weeks later a front-page article in the *New York Times* reported that a big problem for Canada along its border with the United States was the huge number of Americans with fake Canadian medical ID cards coming north for treatment. These were Americans with no health insurance; a cottage industry had sprung up making these fake IDs for them.

I used to live in Europe and have received medical care under the government systems in Belgium, France, and Britain. In no case did I ever feel slighted or the victim of a noncaring bureaucracy. In fact, doctors in these countries routinely make house calls to people who are shut-ins or otherwise have trouble getting out. That kind of personal service is simply not available anymore in most of America.

Many people say they don't want the government involved because it might limit or ration their health care. Yet these same people are often willing to accept without a peep sometimes far more draconian limitations from for-profit health insurance companies and corporations. These restrictions can include shortened hospital stays; surgical procedures on a cheaper, outpatient basis; and unrealistic limitations on drugs and services. There is often little recourse to these limits, whereas government agencies are more directly subject to political pressures from elected officials who in turn are more responsive to public opinion.

Who Has More Choice?

Stephen L. Wyss, the managing director of Affinity Group Underwriters in Glen Allen, Virginia, is an insurance executive whose views are contrary to many in his industry. "The health insurance problem in this country is not going to be solved fully by the private sector," he said. "It probably has a social solution, not a private-sector solution."

Wyss, an American who lived in Canada for nine years, praises that country's national health plan and says people in the United States have a distorted view of it. "The common view here is that Canadians hate their system and want to come down here," he said. "But you talk to Canadians and you won't find that at all. There is a wait for elective procedures, no doubt, but not for serious things. There are very few in Canada who would trade their system for ours. Among the population, support for the principles of universal health care is exceedingly strong. They recognize that they don't have 40 million uninsured people."

He said it is a common misconception here that in Canada you have to go to a doctor you don't choose. "The Canadian system has complete freedom of choice in doctors," he said.

Wyss said some Canadian doctors want to come to the United States because they think they can make more money. "They can be noisy and visible," he said. "So the picture we have here is of underpaid disgruntled doctors who don't take care of you. It just isn't like that. When I lived there, the quality of care was never any different than the quality of care here," he added. "The real difference is how the two countries pay for health care. We pay for it with premiums; they pay for it through taxes."

About ten years ago my father had a second heart-bypass surgery through his Medicare HMO. This was a serious operation that involved opening his chest cavity and repairing his heart while he was on a heart-lung machine. Yet his HMO allowed him only four nights in the hospital. I picked him up on the fifth day and was appalled that he was being discharged. He clearly needed to stay in the hospital a few more days. Yet home he went, shaky and very unsteady on his feet. Luckily, his HMO did pay for a visiting nurse service for a certain amount of time.

A few years later, the father of a Canadian friend had similar surgery in the Toronto area. My friend's father stayed in the hospital for two weeks and then was placed in an extended-care facility for a month before he finally went home.

Although both men's surgeries were successful, wasn't the longer hospital stay and supervised recuperation period safer and more civilized? Who was the more caring provider, the private insurer or the Canadian government? Which way would you like to have your father treated? Or be treated yourself?

Can Boomers Change the Tide?

We have to deal with reality. There's not going to be national health insurance in this country anytime soon; the best we can probably hope for is a patchwork of fixes here and there.

Unfortunately, the problem of people wanting to retire early is not high on any congressional list. With more than 41 million people without any health insurance whatsoever, help for those who are working and have benefits is a hard sell. In 1998 President Clinton proposed allowing uninsured Americans between fifty-five and sixty-four to enroll in Medicare for $3,600 to $5,000 a year, depending on their age—a so-called Medicare buy-in. That proposal went nowhere in Congress.

Some form of national health insurance could solve both of these problems at once. Given the conservative tilt in Washington, however, things are probably going to have to get a whole lot worse before they get better.

Paul Fronstin, an economist and director of the health policy research program at the Employee Benefit Research Institute, a nonprofit and nonpartisan policy organization in Washington, D.C., says future retirees are going to be more hard hit with insurance problems than current retirees. "Employers are changing retiree health benefits, reducing them, or making it harder for people to qualify once they retire," he said. "But they've done just about everything they can to current retirees. The changes are really going to have an effect on the baby boomers as they start to retire. But it's hard to know what will happen. The boomers are such a large group that if they organize they can have an impact on policy, like forcing a Medicare buy-in similar to what Clinton proposed."

How much political clout the boomers will exercise remains to be seen. But because of something that happened in 1989—I call it the Dan Rostenkowski factor—politicians are paying close attention to this aging generation. In the summer of 1989, Rostenkowski, then a congressman from Illinois and the powerful chairman of the House Ways and Means Committee, was besieged by a crowd of fifty senior citizens in Chicago. According to the *Chicago Tribune*, the protesters—shouting "coward," "recall," and "impeach"— forced him to sprint through a gas station to his car, where minutes earlier an elderly demonstrator had been sprawling across the hood.

The protesters were angry about a new law that provided catastrophic coverage for Medicare recipients, but with an income-tax surcharge of up to $800 a year that was set to rise to $1,050 in 1993. That law was soon repealed. The television images of Rostenkowski under assault struck fear in the hearts of politicians that remains to this day. Few want to be pitted against older people on issues involving medical care and Medicare. "Politicians were traumatized by the Rostenkowski episode, and they remain traumatized," said Henry Aaron of the Brookings Institution.

Now many think the worried baby boomers, known for spending instead of saving, will use their political muscle to force changes for their benefit in social programs like Medicare. After all, this is the war-protesting generation that chased Lyndon Johnson out of Washington in the 1960s.

But Neil Howe, the coauthor with William Strauss of *Generations: The History of America's Future, 1584 to 2069* (William Morrow, 1992), doesn't think so. While he agreed that their numbers could give them some influence, "boomers are not particularly effective politically, as an organized lobby for their own collective benefit," he said. "As old people, they will dominate the culture and they will have a lot of personal passion. But that will not translate into anything that's politically effective." He added: "They were throwing rocks in the 1960s because they had no power. But the way you express yourself when you're young and out of power is very different from when you're old and in charge of institutions." So we can't expect legions of elderly boomers to take to the streets, 1960s style? "No, but they'll complain and whine a lot," Howe said.

That should be music to the ears of politicians who remember Dan Rostenkowski. Unless Howe is wrong.

WHEN YOU HAVE TO BUY HEALTH INSURANCE

What do you do if you want to retire and your employer does not provide retiree health benefits? The answer depends on the state of your finances, the state of your health, and the state where you plan to live. The bottom line is that you're going to have to buy health insurance, and it's not going to be cheap. The trick is to make it affordable for you.

Whatever you do, don't allow yourself to be without insurance—not even for a short time. All it takes is the onset of a serious illness or an accident to expose yourself to financial ruin. Better to keep working than to retire with no health insurance if you're too young for Medicare and can't get coverage any other way.

Thanks to some legal safeguards, most early retirees can get insurance—for a price.

The First Step: States Vary

Gary Lauer, the chief executive of eHealthInsurance.com, an online health insurance broker, says dealing with health insurance can be very confusing for most people because they have never had to think much about it. It's always been provided by their employer.

If your employer doesn't provide retiree health benefits—and most don't—you must start thinking about how you'll provide them for yourself if you want to retire early. Your main options are to buy an individual policy on the private market or to extend your employee health insurance for eighteen months under a federal law known as COBRA. These two choices are complicated, however, and carry long-term ramifications. Buying an individual policy can be much less expensive than COBRA, but if you pass on COBRA you will lose some important legal safeguards, including eligibility for post-COBRA coverage under another federal law known as HIPAA. More about this later.

Your access to an individual policy depends to a large degree on where you live. The states have varying laws that govern access to health insurance. Three terms you need to become familiar with are *guaranteed-issue, community rating*, and *preexisting conditions*.

The Blue Cross and Blue Shield Association, a trade group based in Chicago that represents the nation's Blue Cross and Blue Shield plans, lists twelve states with guaranteed-issue laws. The laws vary but generally mean that insurance companies that offer individual policies have to sell you insurance regardless of preexisting conditions, although there can be waiting periods for those with such conditions if you are not switching from current coverage. Usually insurers can't cancel your policy unless they pull out of the market in your state. The twelve states are: Idaho, Iowa, Kentucky, Maine, Massachusetts, New Jersey, New York, Ohio, Rhode Island, South Dakota, Utah, and Vermont. Because the insurers in these twelve states have to take all comers, regardless of preexisting health conditions, the policies can be very expensive. But at least you can get them.

If you are healthy and have no preexisting medical conditions, buying private insurance should not be difficult in a state without guaranteed-issue laws. However, how many people in their mid-fifties and older have no previous medical conditions? A health insurance policy that doesn't cover these conditions can be an invitation to trouble. Even if you get a policy that covers everything, you could face big premium increases if you get sick—again, depending on the state in which you live.

This brings us to community rating. Most states allow insurers to base premiums for individual policies on a client's age and health.

Three states—New Jersey, New York, and Vermont—have pure community rating. This means insurers have to charge everyone the same premium for a particular policy regardless of age or health. Premiums can be raised only for all policyholders; individuals cannot be singled out for increases. Since these three states also have guaranteed-issue laws, there is little competition among insurance companies and prices are high. But again, you can at least get the insurance and you can't be singled out for a rate increase.

Other states, including some of those with guaranteed-issue laws, have lesser degrees of community rating. Some don't have it at all. There are twenty-three states that have neither guaranteed-issue laws nor community rating. These states have the lowest premiums, but you may not be able to get the insurance because insurers are allowed to "cherry pick" the healthiest clients. If you can't get insurance in one of these states you could be forced into high-risk insurance pools with very steep rates and sometimes long waiting lists. The twenty-three states are: Alabama, Alaska, Arizona, Arkansas, California, Colorado, Connecticut, Delaware, Florida, Georgia, Illinois, Kansas, Maryland, Mississippi, Missouri, Montana, Nebraska, Nevada, North Carolina, Oklahoma, South Carolina, Tennessee, and Texas.

A good place to check out prices for individual policies is eHealthInsurance.com's Web site (www.ehealthinsurance.com). You don't have to register and you can browse prices anonymously. All you need to provide is a zip code and a date of birth, and check if you smoke or are a student. If you want to apply for insurance, you can do so online or there is a toll-free number you can call for help and information.

A Tough Choice

Although rates constantly change, I checked some monthly premiums for a traditional plan with a $1,000 to $1,500 annual deductible for a husband and wife, each sixty years old. I looked for plans that would pay 70 to 80 percent of most medical bills, including prescription drug coverage (after deductibles and copayments), with an annual out-of-pocket limit of about $2,000 per person.

The cost of such a plan in New Jersey—one of the guaranteed-issue states with community rating—was more than $2,000 a month. The premiums were often less than half of that amount in states with no guaranteed-issue laws or community rating. But there is no assurance you can get the coverage in the cheaper state or that it will cover preexisting conditions. An HMO in New Jersey—with a $30 co-pay for office visits to a doctor—would cost the same couple about $830 a month; again, in one of the cheaper states the rate could be half that. There are few out-of-pocket expenses in an HMO, but your choice of doctors and hospitals is limited. How restrictive the limits are varies among HMOs.

As you can see, buying an individual health insurance policy is a three-point balancing act based on how much you can spend, your health, and where you live.

The best possible scenario is that your health is good and you live in, or will move to, one of the states with no guaranteed-issue laws or community rating. This will give you the best deal initially. But remember, insurers in these states can raise your rates—sometimes by a lot—if you have a serious illness. If you have health issues, you're probably better off in a state like New Jersey or New York, where insurance and rates are guaranteed, even though it will cost more. Obviously, the worst-case scenario for private insurance is to be in one of these high-cost states on a tight budget. These traditional private policies are clearly not going to work for everybody, so let's look at some other possibilities in building a bridge to Medicare.

The COBRA Option

COBRA, or the Consolidated Omnibus Budget Reconciliation Act, is a federal law that allows you to continue your employee health insurance benefits for eighteen months after you leave your job. That period can be thirty-six months for your spouse if you are eligible for Medicare when you retire but he or she is not. Your spouse is also eligible for thirty-six months if you die or divorce. You must work for a company with twenty or more employees and not have any other insurance or be eligible for Medicare. You can get COBRA even if you have been laid off or fired for any reason other than gross misconduct; you must apply within sixty days.

The great thing about COBRA is that you are guaranteed the coverage, just as though you were working, in any state that is within your plan's coverage area. However, if you are in an employer-sponsored HMO, that coverage area can be limited. If you plan to move away, and your HMO doesn't offer coverage in the new location, you might want to switch to traditional coverage during an enrollment period a year or so before you retire— assuming your company or plan allows it. Otherwise, you could wind up with a COBRA policy that covers only emergency room services, forcing you to travel to your previous area for other medical care. A Long Island woman who retired with HMO coverage under COBRA later moved to Florida and discovered that the only coverage she had there was for emergencies. She was forced to make trips back to New York for checkups and surgery.

The problem with COBRA is that it's expensive, although probably not as high as individual coverage in some guaranteed-issue, community-rated states. Also, what's expensive for a person who has lost his or her job and is out of work may not be expensive for a retiree.

If you accept COBRA, your company can charge you its costs, plus a 2 percent administrative fee. COBRA for a husband and wife can run upward to $1,000 a month, as illustrated by the Taaffe family in chapter 4. Two reasons COBRA is expensive is that your company is no longer picking up most of the tab, and employers must cover all employees, regardless of their health. They can't cherry-pick. It's sort of a corporate version of a guaranteed-issue state.

People with few health problems may find it cheaper to go for an individual policy. That could be a big mistake. By declining COBRA benefits or by using them for only a short time, you may cut off a future path to guaranteed coverage. That's because another advantage of COBRA is that once you exhaust it, you come under another federal law called HIPAA, or the Health Insurance Portability and Accountability Act of 1996. This means that you are eligible for HIPAA plans in every state. Insurers operating in each state must offer two HIPAA-eligible plans, one that is basic and one with broader benefits. These plans cannot differ greatly from other plans an insurer offers. The problem is that they are also expensive because the insurers must accept all applicants. But, again, you are guaranteed the coverage without waiting periods and regardless of preexisting conditions. Note: You must apply for HIPAA coverage within sixty-three days of exhausting COBRA coverage, or you lose your right to do so.

COBRA can be your route to uninterrupted, albeit expensive, coverage until you are eligible for Medicare, especially if you have health problems that may be a barrier to an individual policy. COBRA is also protection against a big jump in premiums if you get sick.

COBRA is more attractive if you have preexisting conditions. If you're healthy, consider a private policy. Even if the premiums do jump, you still may be ahead. But remember, if you forgo COBRA, you also forgo HIPAA eligibility.

Paul Fronstin of the Employee Benefit Research Institute says that most people are better off with non-HIPAA policies if they have no health problems or preexisting conditions. He said that the annual cost of a non-HIPAA plan in Washington, D.C., was about $4,600, compared with $12,000 for a HIPAA plan, for an individual between the ages of fifty-five and sixty-four. The most important thing is to have insurance, one way or another. Fronstin says that people who go without it "are playing Russian roulette with a catastrophic illness."

Other Health Insurance Options

There are some possibilities for getting health insurance other than through COBRA and traditional individual policies:

- Group insurance through an association
- Student insurance
- Catastrophic insurance with a large deductible
- Short-term insurance

Join a Group

Many fraternal organizations or professional associations—so-called affinity groups, many with very lax membership rules—offer group health insurance to their members. Preexisting conditions must be covered, and you can't be singled out for a premium increase. Premiums can be less than those for individual policies, depending on the coverage and where you live.

Insurance coverage through affinity groups, though, can be dicey. Because people with health problems sometimes join an association just to get health coverage, insurers often face a less healthy group than would be the case with a large employer. As a result, insurance companies often drop associations after a year or two, forcing them to scramble for another carrier. Also, some state laws make it very difficult for affinity groups to offer health insurance to their members.

Back to School

Student insurance might seem an odd option for someone looking to retire, but if you want to go back to college—even for a semester—it can be just the ticket: it covers preexisting conditions, and you can keep it when you are no longer a student. To qualify initially, you must usually be classified by a school as a full-time student. For a couple, it could be expensive—depending on the state—since both husband and wife would have to be students and buy the policies individually. The advantage is that it is insurance you can get without question.

"It can be a great solution for a lot of people," said Gary Lauer, the eHealthInsurance.com chief executive. "It's guaranteed-issue, robust insurance. Once you have it, you can keep it for your entire life, whether you graduate or quit after one semester."

Of course, a sixty-one-year-old person heading off to classes is going to pay more for student insurance than a twenty-year-old. The premiums for such polices are usually priced on an annual basis and, of course, vary from state to state.

In Phoenix, for instance, a student policy with a $2,500 deductible would cost a twenty-year-old $492 a year; for a sixty-one-year-old, the price would be $6,744 ($562 a month). Double that for a couple. A similar policy in Chicago would be $574 for the younger student and $3,934 ($328 a month) for the older one. In San Diego, $615 and $8,430 ($703); in Fort Myers, Florida, $656 and $4,496 ($375); and in Denver, $369 and $2,529 ($211). The prices apply statewide in all cases.

Catastrophic Insurance

For those early retirees who are healthy and have a financial cushion, the least expensive route could be a catastrophic plan with a large deductible. Such plans—with annual deductibles of $5,000 to $10,000, and higher—can be 20 to 40 percent, or more, cheaper than traditional low-deductible policies.

Of course, this means that your insurance doesn't kick in until you've spent the deductible. If you do get sick or have an accident, you must be certain you have the resources—that you are, so to speak, self-insured—to cover the deductible amount. "If you are not healthy, this is not a good solution," said Stephen Wyss of Affinity Group Underwriters.

Richard Mayer, the independent financial consultant in Mineola, New York, says catastrophic, or major medical, plans can "absolutely" be a good idea for many retirees who don't yet qualify for Medicare. "As people become more educated about insurance, they'll realize the values of these catastrophic policies," he said. "After all, why do we have health insurance? Not for the little things like a $100 doctor's bill, but for big things like a serious illness or accident."

Gary Lauer of eHealthInsurance.com added: "The purpose of health insurance is to protect against financial disaster. Many of our customers buy catastrophic policies because the premiums are lower and they are willing to self-insure for more mundane health needs like doctor visits and prescriptions."

Here are some sample monthly premiums for a basic $5,000 deductible major medical plan for a sixty-one-year-old man and his sixty-year-old wife in the five cities mentioned earlier:

Phoenix	$279.30
Chicago	$341.00
San Diego	$378.00 ($4,000 deductible)
Fort Myers	$323.00
Denver	$224.00

In New Jersey, where insurance costs are high because it is a guaranteed-issue, community-rated state, Horizon Blue Cross Blue Shield offers a catastrophic policy with an annual $10,000 deductible. After that you would have to pay 50 percent of your bills until you have laid out another $5,000. Then the plan would pay 100 percent. That means you might have to spend up to $15,000 for health care in a given year. The monthly premium for a couple is $477.87; for a single person, it's $198.54. But remember, this is a state where a traditional comprehensive individual plan for a couple can cost more than $2,000 a month and an HMO more than $800.

EHealthInsurance.com and other companies sell health discount cards that can help lower the costs on the deductible portion of a catastrophic policy. EHealthInsurance.com's card is called eHealth. Lauer says the card basically entitles the holder to discounts at participating pharmacies, dentists, physicians, and vision-care specialists that are similar to what large insurance companies negotiate. For prescriptions, the discounts can run up to 13 percent for brand-name drugs and up to 50 percent for generics; dental discounts can be more than 50 percent; physicians, up to 40 percent; and vision care up to 60 percent.

At the eHealthInsurance.com Web site, you can use your zip code to check if your health care provider or pharmacy accepts the cards. Most of the big drug chains do, including Wal-Mart, Rite Aid, and Costco. My dentist does not, but within five miles of my home in New Jersey more than fifty other dentists do. All the doctors I use were listed as accepting the card.

The price of the eHealth card for pharmacy and vision coverage only is $7.95 a month for an individual and $9.95 for a family. Dental coverage only is $7.95 and $9.95. A card covering all three—pharmacy, vision, and dental—is $10.95 and $12.95. Physician coverage cannot be purchased separately, but must be combined with the other three services. That card is $39.95 a month for an individual and $49.95 for a family.

For a healthy retiree with enough savings to absorb a high deductible if necessary, a catastrophic plan combined with one of these health discount cards could prove the least expensive path to Medicare. If you have expensive health problems, look elsewhere.

Short-Term Insurance

Short-term insurance is just that: it's good for periods of from a month up to three years. If you're are old enough, it can be enough to get you to Medicare. "It's a real possibility for some people," said Gary Lauer of eHealthInsurance.com. "For one thing, it's relatively easy to qualify for. It can be great if you're between jobs, on a leave, or filling in a gap until you're eligible for Medicare." He said it could often be a cheaper alternative to COBRA. "We tell COBRA-eligible people to apply for short-term insurance or other private policies," he said. "If you don't qualify, you can always fall back on COBRA."

Some examples of monthly short-term insurance premiums for a couple—he sixty, she sixty-one—in the cities we have used for earlier comparisons are: Phoenix, $262.08; Chicago, $314.50; San Diego, $327.60; Fort Myers, $388.10; and Denver, $327.60. The prices are for policies with a $2,500 deductible.

In March 2002, Theron Scott Johnston, then sixty-four, of Orange, California, received a quarterly bill—due April 1—for $1,500 for his private health insurance. Johnston is a semiretired computer consultant who would turn sixty-five, and be eligible for Medicare, the following August. He knew he was looking at premiums of $3,000 until then. This was for coverage only for himself; his wife was already sixty-five and covered under Medicare.

Johnston had seen some references to short-term insurance on the Internet and wondered if he might be able to save some money with it. He contacted eHealthInsurance.com, where he bought a policy from a company called Fortis. The policy, which would cover him only from April 1 until he turned sixty-five in August, had a $5,000 deductible. But its total cost was a bit less than $600—for the entire period—allowing him to save more than $2,400. "Because of the high deductible, the short-term policy was not as good as my other policy had been," he said. "But I had enough money that I could afford to take the $5,000 gamble on the high deductible. Also, I'm a runner and in very good health. I have no preexisting conditions and take no medication. Nevertheless, before I switched I had a complete physical to be sure." He was quick to add that his switch was only a good move for someone like him who is in good health. "Even if you could afford the deductible, if a preexisting condition is excluded from coverage under a policy, you could face crushing medical bills if you get sick," he said. "But in my case, it was certainly worth the effort."

A Break on Prescriptions

If your health insurance doesn't include prescription drug coverage, you may be eligible for free drugs from pharmaceutical companies. Virtually all the drug makers will provide free medicines for those who have no drug coverage and whose incomes fall below certain levels, regardless of age. The income limits are not that strict—in some cases people earning as much as $50,000 a year can qualify. One unavoidable wrinkle is that you must apply separately to each company that makes your medications. The drugs are commonly dispensed through doctors, and patients usually have to requalify regularly.

The drug companies do not heavily advertise these programs. Even some doctors are unaware of them, and some others don't want to get involved because of the potential paperwork. But the paperwork is really not that onerous. Sometimes it's just one page and must include copies of tax returns or other income documentations. For some patients, these plans can literally be lifesavers. According to a 1998 survey by the *Wall Street Journal*, 80 percent of retirees use a prescription drug every day, and the average Medicare beneficiary needs eighteen prescriptions a year.

There are companies that, for a relatively small fee, will provide information on the various programs offered by the drugmakers, including each company's eligibility requirements. Two are Harsonhill (www.prescriptions4free.com) and the Medicine Program (www.themedicineprogram.com).

While these services can be helpful, you really don't need to pay for this information. The Web site of the Pharmaceutical Research and Manufacturers of America (www.phrma.org) has the same information—free—that is being sold by companies like Harsonhill and the Medicine Program. Drug companies will provide information directly to doctors.

Knowledge and Advice

Health insurance in the United States is complicated, tricky, and expensive. No article or book chapter can do more than scratch the surface. Know the rules and the law. Compare prices and details on the Internet. Ask questions. Before signing on the dotted line for any insurance, ask this question: What does this policy *not* cover? Sometimes the answer to that can be as important as a list of what is covered. Finally, go to an independent insurance broker—or two or three. Independent financial counselors can also help. They often know which companies have reputations for increasing premiums or making it difficult to file claims or delaying payments. The National Association of Health Underwriters (www.nahu.org) can help you find one of their members in your area.

7

Social Security: Count on It

The most important thing we could do to protect
Social Security right now is leave it alone.
—MARK WEISBROT, COAUTHOR,
SOCIAL SECURITY: THE PHONY CRISIS

Many Americans think that the Social Security system is in deep
trouble and needs major fixing or restructuring to "save" it from
going broke. *Looming insolvency* is the term most often used in
the media to describe the system's purported plight. Politicians
issue dire warnings about the graying of America and the threat of
generational warfare. Poll after poll reflects this concern among
citizens; many young people say they expect they will never
receive any Social Security benefits despite years of paying the tax.
Efforts are under way to privatize the system, which would allow
individuals to invest their Social Security taxes in the stock market.

Well, you can stop worrying.

None of these dire predictions is even remotely likely. And privatization might well do more harm than good. So-called reform
of the Social Security system increasingly looks like a solution in
search of a problem. What other issue can you think of, with a

problem forty years down the road, that has politicians equally engaged?

Even under relatively gloomy economic forecasts, Social Security is rock-solid for about four decades, until 2042. With some minimal changes, it will be fine until 2077 or perhaps until the end of the century. That's assuming future economic growth is just half the annual average of about 3.5 percent over the last seventy-five years.

"The most important thing we could do to protect Social Security right now is leave it alone," said Mark Weisbrot, codirector of the Center for Economic and Policy Research in Washington, D.C., and coauthor with Dean Baker of *Social Security: The Phony Crisis* (University of Chicago Press, 2001).

Why all the fuss? Think hidden agendas, on all sides.

THE PUSH FOR PRIVATIZATION

Wall Street and its commission-driven brokers would love to get their hands on at least some of the $1.4 trillion in the Social Security trust fund, which is currently invested in United States government bonds. In its January 2002 issue, *Harper's Magazine* published an essay by Thomas Frank titled "The Trillion-Dollar Hustle: Hello Wall Street, Goodbye Social Security." It's an excellent short primer on Wall Street's push for privatization.

In addition, ultraconservative Republicans and others who are ideologically opposed to the whole concept of government-sponsored social insurance would like to fully privatize the system. Knowing that idea won't fly politically, they are pushing for partial privatization, in which individuals would invest a portion of their Social Security tax in the stock market, all in the name of rescuing the system. The concept has picked up some support across the political spectrum, although it lost a bit of steam as the stock market went south after the boom years of the 1990s. Several variations remain under consideration, including one modeled after individual retirement accounts; it would give Americans broad discretion over how they invested their money.

The immediate problem with privatization is that Social Security is a pay-as-you-go system: today's retirees are supported by today's workers. The surplus in the trust fund is there to handle the bulge in the retiree population that will occur when the large numbers of baby boomers soon begin to retire. Partial privatization would take up to a third of current revenues and put the money into private accounts. How would this money—upward of $200 billion a year—be replaced so that current benefits could be paid? The government could increase taxes, take on more debt, or cut benefits—all unpleasant solutions to a problem that didn't need to be created in the first place.

Proponents of privatization don't like to be reminded that, as we have seen in recent years, stocks can go down as well as up. Weisbrot, an economist, points out that declines can be long-term. Between 1968 and 1978, for example, the stock market lost 45 percent of its value. He and the Center for Economic and Policy Research (www.cepr.net) have calculated that if the most modest of the various privatization plans had been put into effect at the beginning of 1998, by November 1, 2002, the Social Security system would have lost $45 billion.

We'll look at some other difficulties with privatization later.

Bipartisan "Concern"

The exaggerations about Social Security's problems are coming not just from Republicans and other conservatives. Remember President Clinton exhorting Congress to use the budget surplus to "save" Social Security instead of cutting taxes? The Democrats try to score political points by depicting themselves as the great saviors of Social Security. The Republicans aren't about to cry foul and say the system doesn't need saving. If they do, there goes their argument for privatization. "There's a kind of gentlemen's agreement here in Washington, I'm afraid, not to point out the basic fact that we don't really need to be talking about Social Security," Weisbrot said.

One of the biggest smoke screens in the debate is the idea that the Social Security "crisis" will cause generational conflicts as younger people are forced to support a growing older population. The argument conjures up images of old people with canes and walkers, barricaded in retirement villages, fighting off roving hoards of Generation Xers and Yers. Ari Fleischer, the former White House press secretary, said in a 2002 press briefing that as Social Security is currently structured, younger workers paying into the system would "get nothing back." He was later forced to retract that statement when some economists pointed out that it was in direct contradiction to the Social Security trustees' annual report.

It's important to keep in mind that, as Knight A. Kiplinger writes in *World Boom Ahead: Why Business and Consumers Will Prosper* (Kiplinger Books, 1998), the graying of America will be very gradual. It may be true that by 2020 about 53 million people, or 16 percent of the population, will be over sixty-five, compared with the current 35 million, or 12.4 percent. But Kiplinger says that isn't the whole picture. Because of general population growth, including immigration, the number of young people will be growing, too, and the nation's median age in 2020 will be 38.1, slightly less than the median age of Florida's current population: about 38.7. The current national median age is 35.3.

Moreover, Generation Xers and Yers didn't spring full-grown from the mind of Tommy Hilfiger. They have parents and grandparents, too, and they want them to have secure retirements. Today's young people themselves will eventually retire. Polls by the 2030 Center, which studies economic issues affecting younger people, show broad support by young people for Social Security.

Here's a modest proposal. Since whatever problems Social Security may have are a very long way off, let's have a ten-year test of privatization—with congressional pensions. Let Congress pass a law linking representatives' and senators' pensions to the Standard & Poor's 500 stock index. Maybe as Congress debates health care, it should force its members into HMOs. Both moves would, to borrow from Dr. Johnson, focus their minds wonderfully.

Good News from the Trustees

Every year the trustees of Social Security issue an annual report on the status of the system. The report covering 2002 was issued on Monday, March 17, 2003—the day President Bush gave Saddam Hussein an ultimatum to leave Iraq within forty-eight hours. Two days later the war began.

The report was little noticed in the media, which was busy covering the conflict. That's unfortunate, because the trustees had some good news. They extended by a year two important deadlines when Social Security's critics say the system faces real trouble:

- The projected point at which tax revenues will fall below expenses, forcing the system to dip into its trust fund to pay benefits, was moved to 2018 from 2017.
- The point at which the trust fund will be exhausted was put at 2042, instead of 2041 as cited in last year's report.

Oddly, the headline on the news release summarizing the report—"Social Security Not Sustainable for the Long Term"—seemed a tad pessimistic, given that a trustee report as recently as 1995 had put the date for the trust fund to be depleted at 2030. That's twelve years earlier than is expected in the 2003 report.

Sure, it is technically true that if nothing changes—if Social Security taxes are never increased no matter how much the economy grows—and if all economic and demographic projections are perfectly on target, then in 2042 the system will be able to pay out only 73 percent of scheduled benefits. That's a lot of ifs spread out over almost four decades.

The trustees' report actually peers seventy-five years into the future. To fill the gap created by the expiration of the trust fund in 2042 and keep the system going until 2077 would require an additional $3.5 trillion. That's $200 billion more than was estimated in last year's report.

That sounds like a lot of money, but it covers a seventy-five-year period. To put it in perspective, if we increased Social Security taxes today to fill that $3.5 trillion gap, the rise would have to be 1.92 percentage points, half to be paid by workers and half by employers. That would mean each would pay 7.16 percent; they now pay 6.2 percent. Of course, the longer we wait, the steeper the increase would have to be.

Raising the payroll tax is not the only alternative, however. Such an increase could be less if it were combined with an increase in the amount of a person's annual income that is subject to Social Security taxes. The ceiling for 2003, for example, was $87,000; if you earned more than that it was free of Social Security taxes. But raising the ceiling and making the tax less regressive would involve raising taxes on wealthier people—not a popular idea in Washington these days.

"If you were going to take the current system and fix it but not in a structural way—a little bit of this and a little bit of that—then raising the ceiling could certainly be in the mix," said John L. Palmer, one of two appointed public trustees for Social Security and Medicare. "It would increase benefits somewhat because they are calculated on a person's taxable base. But, on balance, it would improve the finances of the system. And it would make the tax more progressive."

All this, of course, is based on very long-term projections by a government that often has had trouble predicting budget surpluses and deficits a year or two in advance. "There is a tremendous amount of uncertainty in a seventy-five-year projection," conceded Palmer, who is an economist and the dean of the Maxwell School of Citizenship and Public Affairs at Syracuse University.

Mark Weisbrot of the Center for Economic and Policy Research says the idea of making predictions seventy-five years into the future is a "joke." "You may as well use a crystal ball," he said. "It's science fiction."

One Washington wag put it more bluntly: "Anybody who thinks they can make economic projections for seventy-five years from now ought not to be allowed on the street unassisted."

John Palmer says a lot of analysis goes into the Social Security projections, which fall mid-range between optimistic and pessimistic outlooks. However, there are plenty of economists who think the Social Security projections are based on estimates that are too conservative. This is important because if future economic growth is greater than projected by even a little, it has profoundly positive consequences for Social Security. The expected shortfalls can shrink or even vanish if growth is sufficient. Jeremy J. Siegel, a professor of finance at the Wharton School of the University of Pennsylvania and the author of *Stocks for the Long Run: The Definitive Guide to Financial Market Returns and Long-Term Investment Strategies* (McGraw-Hill, 2002), agrees that economic growth could go a long way toward solving Social Security's problems. Nevertheless, he favors partial privatization, not because it will rescue the system but because he thinks it will encourage people to save.

It's not just the economy the trustees' projections take into account. "A big driver for our long-term projections are birth rates and life expectancy," Palmer said. Lower birth rates and longer life expectancy mean that there will be fewer young people paying into the system and those collecting benefits will collect them longer. Immigration is an important factor that can help offset declining birth rates. Palmer said a major reason the 2003 report moved those two dates forward by a year was a higher assumption about immigration over the next fifteen to twenty years, based on the 2000 census.

The Government Borrowed Our Money

The Social Security system pays benefits out of current taxes with the surplus going into a trust fund, so there will be money available for the expected increase in future retirees as the baby boomers start collecting benefits in a few years. That trust fund, which is invested in government bonds and is often misunderstood, has become a political football. Its expected depletion is cited by critics who want to "save" Social Security by privatizing it, or are ideologically opposed to the concept of government-sponsored social insurance. That the fund is expected to start redeeming its bonds in 2018 to help pay benefits is often decried as a huge problem for Social Security because the payout will come from the Treasury.

That's not Social Security's problem. It's a fiscal problem for the government, which has borrowed the money by issuing the bonds. Through 2002, the fund contained nearly $1.4 trillion in bonds, which earned interest of 6.4 percent that year—or $80.4 billion. If Congress doesn't want to repay the money, it shouldn't have borrowed it. To see the redemption of those bonds as Social Security's problem is akin to borrowing money from a bank and then, when the debt comes due, declaring it the bank's problem. Palmer agreed with that assessment, but noted that the exhaustion of the trust funds in 2042 would be a Social Security problem. Also, the bonds aren't all going to be cashed in at once. They'll be gradually redeemed by Social Security as needed over two decades, assuming the projections are correct. If the past is any guide, the dates when the system is expected to face problems may continue to be extended.

Viewing those bonds as a Social Security problem also flirts with the assumption that the government might default on them, something that has never happened in the nation's history. A lot of people own government bonds; some rich people own a lot of them. "Ross Perot has invested in U.S. Treasury bonds, and nobody is talking about his not being paid," said Mark Weisbrot of the Center for Economic and Policy Research. "Why should 150 million workers be treated any differently? These Social Security bonds carry the full faith and credit of the government. If they're not going to be paid, you may as well throw away that $20 bill in your pocket." He added: "The government took the money out of our checks, and put it in bonds. They happen to be government bonds. What if Social Security had invested this money in private corporate bonds? We wouldn't even be having this discussion. They would just be cashed in. Why should this be any different?"

Not a New Problem

Weisbrot also thinks the Social Security system is basically in good shape and that future problems will be minor and readily solved. "By 2042 people will be making more than 40 percent above what they make today, in real inflation-adjusted terms, according to the trustees' own projections," he said. "Is anyone really worried about paying an additional 1 percent of their income for a system that keeps our old people out of poverty? Maybe people who are ideologically opposed to the concept. But the Social Security tax has been raised by more than this in the past. The projected shortfalls are less than the shortfalls that were taken care of in the '50s, '60s, '70s, and '80s. The system is more sound than it's been throughout most of its sixty-seven-year history. These shortfall projections are based on the assumption that no taxes will ever be raised, no matter how rich the country gets over the next seventy-five years. That's three-quarters of a century. It's only under that assumption that you can say Social Security has any problem at all."

He said the entire projected shortfall for the next seventy-five years is less than 0.75 percent of our nation's gross domestic product—the total value of all goods and services—over the same period. "We have solved shortages before and there's every indication people would be willing to do it again," he said. "After all, it's not that it's such a small percentage of our income, but that our incomes are going to be so much higher that nobody will ever notice the difference. There's no possibility that anyone is going to suffer a reduced living standard if we have to fill that shortfall in the science fiction future."

He added: "People are being deceived. People who are leading the debate are being deceptive. I just wish the critics would be honest and tell people there is a small problem forty years down the road that can be easily fixed. That shortfall will be taken care of like those in the past. If it weren't for the powerful influence of Wall Street, which wants the commissions privatization would bring, and politically active ideologues, this wouldn't even be an issue."

The Perils of Privatization

The biggest, immediate, and most obvious problem with privatization is the deficit that would be created in the pay-as-you-go system as funds are diverted to private accounts.

The second obvious problem, as I mentioned, is that stocks fall as well as rise. Proponents of privatization often say that over the long term stocks are the best investment because they will deliver higher returns than bonds. Jeremy Siegel of the Wharton School expects market returns to be 5 to 7 percent, adjusted for inflation, over the next decade or so. Sometimes you see predictions of 11 or 12 percent, but they are almost always not adjusted for inflation. In truth, nobody can predict the future of the stock market. Who in the late 1980s saw the market surge of the Clinton boom years of the 1990s?

Of course, investing for the long term is theoretically supposed to smooth out these bumps in the stock market. But your definition of long term depends on your age and when you plan to retire. If you dumped your savings into the stock market in the summer of 1929, you had better have been pretty young. The market's recovery from the October 1987 crash was much faster than from 1929's, but that wasn't much help if you had planned to retire that fall.

In their book *The Great 401(k) Hoax: Why Your Family's*

Financial Security Is at Risk, and What You Can Do About It (Perseus Publishing, 2002), William Wolman and Anne Colamosca say that history suggests we face a stock market slump that could last for two decades. They expect annual returns over these years to average less than 2 percent, adjusted for inflation. That projection makes the Social Security trust fund's investment in government bonds, which paid 6.4 percent in 2002, look pretty sweet.

Winners and Losers

There are other, less obvious problems with privatization that are rooted in the kind of society we are, or aspire to be. Privatization, in which people would be free to invest some of their Social Security taxes in stocks as they wish, would inevitably create a system of winners and losers. Not all people are equally sophisticated at picking stocks or mutual funds. A Century Foundation project on Social Security has pointed out that without the system's guaranteed monthly benefits, about half the elderly in America would fall below the poverty line. Social Security was created to give everyone a base line, a solid floor of income protection. It has been one of the most successful social programs in our nation's history, keeping millions from falling into poverty. Retiree benefits are fully insured against market risks. Do we really want to create a society in which retirees' proximity to the poverty line is determined by their stock market savvy?

Besides retirement income, the Social Security system provides other benefits that could be at risk under privatization. These include insurance to support survivors of workers who die young, guaranteed income for the disabled, and protection from inflation through benefits that are indexed to rise with the cost of living. Also, the cost of administering the Social Security system is much less than private insurers and investment companies charge.

A privatized system would surely have to have some safeguards to protect novice investors from dangers like account-churning by commission-driven brokers. Or brokers who push dubious stock on which they receive an enhanced commission. ("What, you never heard of Southern Indiana Drywall? Well, a lot of people hadn't heard of Microsoft when it got started.") The Century Foundation has suggested that in order to protect workers from losing their retirement funds, most high-risk and novel investments should be ruled out. The catch-22 of such safeguards is that they might restrict people who are really good at investing. This entire proposal clearly needs more thought.

During the 2000 presidential campaign, the Democratic nominee, Vice President Al Gore, was ridiculed for his repetitious pleas for a Social Security "lockbox" to protect the trust fund. Actually, that sideshow obscured his own privatization proposal that made a lot of sense. Gore suggested that we leave the basic Social Security system as it is to maintain a solid base for all retirees. Then he proposed using the budget surplus (remember that?) to fund what he called a Retirement Savings Plus program. Depending on income, people would get tax credits of $500 to $1,500 that would help them establish individual accounts that could be privately invested in mutual funds. The Gore campaign estimated that at the end of thirty-five years, a couple making less than $30,000 would have a retirement nest egg of $400,000—on top of, not instead of, Social Security.

The Gore proposal would have given us the best of both worlds. And it had the added advantage of distributing a tax cut more equally. Such a plan, however, was and remains unpopular with ideologues who are opposed to government-sponsored social insurance no matter how it is structured. They want the government out of Social Security altogether.

Gore did not become president; under President Bush the surplus has been used to fund tax cuts favoring higher-income Americans. That, combined with the expense of war, made black-ink budgets a memory—along with the Gore proposal. President Bush has continued to push for a partial privatization plan.

A More Productive Workforce

One of the most popular arguments used by critics of Social Security is that the number of workers available to support one retiree is declining to a dangerously low, and ultimately unsupportable, level. It is 3.3 today and is expected to drop to 2.2 by 2030. In 1945, there were 41.9 workers for each retiree; in 1955, 8.6; and in 1965, 4.0. From 1975 until 2002, the number remained fairly constant at 3.2 to 3.4. Projections by Social Security trustees call for the numbers to drop to 2.6 in 2020, 2.2 in 2030, 2.1 in 2040, and 1.8 in 2080.

However, as Weisbrot and Baker point out in *Social Security: The Phony Crisis*, these demographic and labor force statistics look scary because they are presented in isolation, out of context relative to other economic factors—and thus more or less meaningless.

First, the authors say, we should look at the reduced burden workers will face as the birth rate declines. They write: "The increase in the future burden of caring for a larger elderly population will be offset to a large extent by the reduced costs of education, child care, and other expenses of caring for dependent children."

Second, they argue, these dire dependency ratios fail to take into account productivity increases. "To say that Social Security will go broke because of the declining number of workers per retiree is like saying that we should be very hungry right now because the percentage of the workforce in agriculture has declined from 5.1 to 1.1 over the last forty years," they write. "Just as we can now feed the nation and in fact export a large agricultural surplus with vastly fewer people employed in agriculture, it is also true that fewer workers can support a large number of retirees as the productivity of the entire economy grows."

The authors also say that the projected decline from 3.3 today to 2.2 in 2030 is less steep than the decline from 8.6 in 1955 to 3.3—and that drop did not precipitate an economic disaster.

Why Roll the Dice?

As the politicians and lobbyists in Washington strive to score political or ideological points in the Social Security debate, they should be aware that people like Edith Chvala are watching them. Like some economists, she questions the wisdom of staking Social Security funds on the stock market. Chvala, eighty, lives alone in a mobile home seven miles southeast of Silver City, New Mexico, on $1,345 a month—$1,184 from Social Security and $161 from a pension.

As she watches the struggle over Social Security, Chvala has come to at least one conclusion: she is not excited about proposals that would put a portion of the funds, now invested in Treasury securities, into the stock market—whether it's a plan for the government to invest the money or one allowing individuals to invest part of their Social Security tax payments themselves. "I'm not a gambler," she said. "It seems like they want to gamble with our retirement money."

A native of Germany, Chvala came to the United States in 1930, when she was seven. She grew up in New York City, living in Queens and then Sheepshead Bay, Brooklyn. She married in 1945 and followed her husband, a construction worker, around the Northeast. In 1970, they moved to Buffalo, New York, where she worked as a nurse's aid for twenty years. That job was the source of her small pension. The couple divorced in 1973; her former husband has since died.

At the urging of a son who lived in New Mexico, she moved there in 1990. She used her savings to buy a mobile home and park it rent-free on property owned by her son and daughter-in-law. The couple later divorced and the son moved to Arizona, but his former wife allowed Chvala to stay. Recent health problems have forced Chvala to curtail her activities, although she continues to drive her 1985 Chevy Blazer. "I like my independence," she said. "My plan is just to drop dead—when the time comes." And in the meantime she would rather that politicians keep their hands off Social Security.

If You Were a Carpenter

Another move often suggested by Social Security's critics is to raise the retirement age to seventy or older for collecting full benefits. The argument is that people are living and working longer, and increasing the retirement age would save money for the system.

Whenever I hear policy strategists or ivory-tower academics proposing this, I can't help wishing they would get up from their ergonomically designed chairs and spend a day with some construction workers at a job site.

I recently talked to a carpenter and a laborer—both in their late thirties—working among the rising girders of an office building in New Jersey. Their jobs are physically difficult, especially during the winter cold. And in their circle of workers, the idea of staying on the job until seventy is not exactly catching fire. "By the time you reach fifty-five or sixty in the heavy construction business, most contractors don't want you," the carpenter said. "You just can't do the hard work after years of getting banged around." The laborer pointed to a huge supermarket nearby. "The blocks they used to build that with weigh a hundred and five pounds each," he said. "I lifted ninety percent of them."

Both the carpenter and the laborer said there was pressure from contractors to keep working hard all day. "I've been on jobs where they get mad if you take too many drinks of water," the carpenter said. "It's go, go, go. If you don't feel good and slack off, that's no excuse." They work, often outside, in rain and snow. And they get paid only if they work. "There are no paid holidays, no vacation, no sick days," he said.

The two men also cited safety as an especially acute issue for older construction workers. The laborer should know. When he was twenty-nine, a scaffold on which he was working collapsed, sending him crashing twenty feet to a concrete floor. He suffered head injuries, his back was broken in three places, and his collarbone was fractured. "If I'd been sixty-six or sixty-seven, I'd have been done for," he said.

You don't have to spend much time talking with people like these two who build our buildings, pave our roads, or tote our trash to see clearly the contrast between them and people who work in comfortably heated and air-conditioned offices. Guess where those who make the retirement-policy decisions work.

The notion of retiring at sixty-five is already slipping away, at least as far as Social Security is concerned. Changes made by Congress in 1983 are ratcheting up the retirement age for people born after 1937 (see figure 5). Of course, no matter when you were born you can get permanently reduced Social Security payments at age sixty-two. Someone born in 1944 must wait an extra year, until they are sixty-six, to get full retirement benefits. If they work in an office, it won't be such a big deal to roll up to their keyboard for another year. But if they operate a jackhammer . . . "A big part of the push to increase the retirement age to seventy is simply that the policy crowd doesn't work at jobs in which they're spent by the time they're sixty-five," Weisbrot said. So the next time you hear someone calling for raising the retirement age to seventy, ask them what they do for a living.

UNDERSTANDING THE SYSTEM

Joe and Sue Sample, the hypothetical couple in chapter 2, plan to retire when they are sixty, but cannot begin collecting even reduced Social Security benefits until they are sixty-two. They cannot collect full benefits until they are sixty-six. (The full retirement age is from sixty-five to sixty-seven, depending on when you were born.)

However, if they stop working at sixty—or take part-time jobs or jobs that pay less than their former positions—they could face an even further, although perhaps slight, reduction in benefits, depending on their work history. That's because monthly benefits are based on an average of your highest thirty-five years of earnings, which are indexed for inflation to bring them up to current dollar amounts. If you don't have thirty-five years, zeros are used for each year you lack. Assuming that the Samples had thirty-three years of work and stopped working at sixty, when they applied for benefits at sixty-two, those last two years would count as zeros in calculating the average on which their benefits are based. Of course, if they had thirty-five years of work, there would be no zeros added. Even with thirty-five years of work, these final years can still be important if, like most people, your highest earning years are at the end of your career.

The longer you wait to retire, the greater your Social Security benefits will be. You just won't be able to collect them for as long. If you need the benefits as soon as possible, like the Samples, to make retirement work for you, then you have no choice. Remember, however, that if you take reduced benefits, they are reduced forever.

Figure 5

Social Security and Retirement Age

Changes to Social Security rules are gradually raising the age at which you may retire and receive full retirement benefits. You may still choose to retire sooner—starting at age 62—but, if you do, your benefits will be reduced according to a formula. Here are the minimum ages for full benefits, depending on the year in which you were born. (People born on January 1 are counted under the previous year.)

For people who were born in:	The **minimum age** to receive full benefits at retirement is:	The amount your benefits is reduced fo **each month** earlier that you retire:	The total reduction if you retire at age 62:
1937 or before	65	0.555%	20.00%
1938	65 years, 2 months	0.548	20.83
1939	65 years, 4 months	0.541	21.67
1940	65 years, 6 months	0.535	22.50
1941	65 years, 8 months	0.530	23.33
1942	65 years, 10 months	0.525	24.17
1943–1954	66	0.520	25.00
1955	66 years, 2 months	0.516	25.84
1956	66 years, 4 months	0.512	26.66
1957	66 years, 6 months	0.509	27.50
1958	66 years, 8 months	0.505	28.33
1959	66 years, 10 months	0.502	29.17
1960 or after	67	0.500	30.00

Source: Social Security Administration

Also remember that if you take benefits at sixty-two, these benefits can be reduced even more if you work and your earnings exceed a specified amount; at your full retirement age, the earnings limit ends. If you have enough money to retire and get by without Social Security, then you have a decision: take the benefits now or wait until you are older and they have grown considerably. Figure 5 shows when you can collect full retirement benefits and the penalty for retiring early.

In Joe Sample's case, for instance, at sixty-two he will get about $1,300 a month. If he waits until he is sixty-six, he'll get about $1,800 a month; at seventy, about $2,500. (For Sue, the figures are $900, $1,300, and $1,800.) However, these projected amounts are based on the assumption that Joe continues working until he collects them. If he retires and holds off taking the benefits, they'll grow somewhat less because of the thirty-five-year averaging. He will miss out on a few years of higher earnings in his average or face some zeros in his average if he falls short of thirty-five years.

In the boom years of the 1990s, when the stock market was making impressive gains, many financial advisers were saying that people should take the benefits as soon as possible, even if they didn't need them, and invest the money. They figured you would be ahead of the game compared with leaving the money in the system and collecting an enhanced benefit when you were older. Now, with the bear market, that advice has pretty much been reversed. That's because if you were born in 1943 or later, the system will increase your retirement benefits 8 percent for every year you delay taking them until you are seventy. In the 1990s, 8 percent was considered a paltry return compared with the stock market; today, it's darned good.

The Social Security Web site (www.ssa.gov) has some online calculators to help you figure out which course is best. Just go to the home page and click on "Online Services."

The Basics of Social Security

The Social Security Web site provides a wealth of information about how the system works and its benefits to you. Its data is rock-solid and accepted (although interpreted differently) by all sides in the debate over the future of the system. Your annual statement showing your earnings record and estimated benefits is also of great value.

Here are some Social Security facts—all explained in greater detail on the Web site—that you should be clear on:

- The tax you pay for Social Security is 6.2 percent of your income, up to an annual limit that was $87,000 in 2003. Your employer pays another 6.2 percent, for a total of 12.4 percent. If you are self-employed, you must pay the entire 12.4 percent.
- That annual salary limit for Social Security taxes rises each year based on increases in the national average wage.
- If you take early retirement benefits at sixty-two, they will be reduced by a percentage that depends on the age at which you are eligible for full benefits. The closer you are to full-benefit age, the less they are reduced. If your full retirement age is sixty-five, and you retire at sixty-two, your monthly benefits will be reduced by about 20 percent; at sixty-three, about 13.3 percent; and at sixty-four, about 6.7 percent. If your full retirement age is sixty-seven, and you retire at sixty-two, your benefits will be lowered by 30 percent; at sixty-three, 25 percent; at sixty-four, 20 percent; at sixty-five, 13.5 percent; and at sixty-six, 6.7 percent.
- If you retire early and decide to take a part-time job or freelance on your own, be wary of some short-term limits on earnings that will reduce your Social Security benefits. If you are less than your full retirement age, $1 in benefits will be deducted for each $2 you earn above an annual limit that was $11,520 in 2003. In the year you reach your full retirement age, $1 in benefits will be deducted for each $3 you earn above a more generous limit that was $30,720 in 2003. In the month you hit full retirement age, all

limits disappear; you can earn as much as you want with no bene-fit reductions. Obviously, if you plan to work in retirement and will have enough money to live on, you might be better off delay-ing collecting Social Security until your full retirement age.

- You can collect Social Security benefits if you live abroad. However, you generally cannot have access to Medicare benefits overseas.

Your Social Security Statement

Pay particular attention to the annual statement you receive from the Social Security Administration. You can also request a state-ment anytime from the Social Security Web site.

The annual statement shows your earnings record. It can be a trip down memory lane. My statement shows that in 1959, when I was a high school freshman, I earned $358. I think that was from working for a public library in Indiana.

The statement also shows what your monthly benefits will be at age sixty-two and at your full retirement age, based on your earn-ings history and the assumption that you continue working until you retire. It also shows how much you would get right now if you were disabled, as well as what your family's benefits would be if you died. People I talked to who haven't paid much attention to their annual statement are often pleasantly surprised by the amounts they'll receive. Some even start thinking about early retirement.

Putting It All Together

I either answer their questions or tell them where they can get answers.
—JIM MILLER, COLUMNIST, "THE SAVVY SENIOR"

Richard Mayer, the Mineola, New York, financial consultant, stresses the importance of looking closely at your financial situation before you make retirement decisions. To that end, he has provided blueprints for calculating expenses and net worth. He separates expenses into five broad categories: automobile, home, insurance, personal, and taxes. He then calculates expense items under each category three ways: preretirement; postretirement in your current location; and postretirement in a new, and presumably less expensive, location. Many preretirement expenses will be less or disappear altogether when you retire, especially if you move to the cheaper location. This is especially true for mortgage payments, multiple car expenses, and taxes. Figure 6 allows you to work through the three scenarios with your own numbers. To calculate expenses in a new location, use data provided by www.BestPlaces.net and www.Retirement Living.com.

Figure 7 allows you to calculate your net worth. At the end of the chart, debts must be subtracted from total assets to arrive at your bottom line.

Finally, of course, you need to calculate your retirement income, much as the Samples did in chapter 2. The value of first charting your net worth is that you may be able to see ways to use some of it to produce income. For instance, if you sell an expensive house and move to a cheaper property, you may have some money left over. You might want to use it to buy an annuity or some other kind of income-producing investment. Although pension income continues to shrink as companies cut back and force employees to rely more on 401(k) plans, for most people the three sources of income in retirement will be a pension, Social Security, and income from investments, including 401(k) plans.

Now you need to put it all together. You know your monthly expenses whether you retire and stay put or move to a new place. You know your net worth. And you know your income. Does it work?

"WHY DIDN'T I THINK OF THAT?"

I decided to end this book with an account of Jim Miller because he is a perfect illustration of the value of a clever idea; the importance of following your bliss, as Joseph Campbell advises; and the value of thinking small. Miller was the subject of my "Seniority" column in the *New York Times* on February 9, 2003, under the heading "The Senior Discount, as Applied by a Writer." One reader lamented in an e-mail, "Why didn't I think of that?"

Miller, forty, of Norman, Oklahoma, writes a weekly, self-syndicated column called "The Savvy Senior" that runs in more than four hundred mostly small daily and weekly newspapers around the country. Here's the part about thinking small: he charges $3 to $5 a week for his column, depending on a paper's circulation.

Figure 6

Worksheet: Monthly Expenses

	Before retiring	After retiring (same location)	After retiring (new location)
Automobile expenses			
Loan or lease payment			
Fuel			
Repairs			
License and registration			
Other			
Expenses for your home			
Mortgage or rent payment			
Electric service			
Gas service			
Fuel oil			
Cable/satellite TV service			
Telephone service—local			
Long distance calling			
Mobile phone			
Water			
Lawn and landscaping			
Association dues			
Other			
Taxes			
Federal income tax			
State income tax			
County income tax			
City income tax			
Real estate tax			
Sewer tax			
Water tax			
School tax			
Other			
Subtotal for this page			

(continued)

Worksheet: Monthly Expenses

	Before retiring	After retiring (same location)	After retiring (new location)
Personal expenses			
Allowance/spending money			
Boat			
Charitable giving			
Clothing and shoes			
Continuing education			
Computer and related			
Cosmetics			
Credit card payments			
Dry cleaning			
Hair care			
Hobbies			
Jewelry			
Club memberships			
Professional dues			
Travel			
Second home			
Subscriptions			
Pets and veterinary			
Food:			
At home			
Restaurants			
Gifts:			
Birthdays			
Holidays			
Other gifts			
Other expenses			
Subtotal for this page			

(continued)

Worksheet: Monthly Expenses

	Before retiring	After retiring (same location)	After retiring (new location)
Insurance			
Automobile			
Homeowners			
Life insurance			
Long-term care			
Mortgage			
Umbrella			
Health:			
Doctor and surgical			
Hospital			
Prescriptions			
Unreimbursed:			
Copayments			
Deductibles			
Dental			
Eyes and glasses			
Hearing			
Medicines			
Other			
Subtotal for this page			
Subtotal from first page			
Subtotal from second page			
Grand total			

Source: Richard E. Mayer

Figure 7

Worksheet: Net Worth

	Bank	Brokerage	Credit union	Life insurance	Total
Cash and liquid assets					
Checking					
Savings					
Money market					
C.D.s					
Treasuries					
Cash value					
Bonds					
Stocks					
Mutual funds					
Annuities					
I.R.A.s					
401(k)					
403(b)					
457					
Profit sharing					
Money purchase					
Pension					
Other accounts					
Subtotal: Cash and liquid assets					

	Estimated value			Estimated value
Personal assets				
Artwork		Jewelry		
Antiques		Collectibles		
Furniture and furnishings		Others		
Precious metals				
Subtotal: Personal assets				

	Gross value	Less: Money owed to other parties	Net value
Businesses and partnerships			
C Corporations			
Partnerships			
Sole proprietor			
Subtotal: Businesses and partnerships			

(continued)

Worksheet: Net Worth

	Gross value	Less: amount of loan outstanding	Net value
Major assets with outstanding debts			
Primary residence			
Second residence			
Unimproved land			
Rental property			
Boat			
R.V.			
Automobiles			
Subtotal: Major assets with outstanding loans			

	Amount owed		Amount owed
Other debts			
Lines of credit		Federal taxes	
Life insurance loans		State taxes	
Credit card balances		Local taxes	
Student loans		Other	
Personal loans			
Other loans			
Subtotal: Other debts			

Adding it all up			
From first page:	Cash and liquid assets		
	Personal assets		
	Businesses and partnerships		
From this page:	Major assets with outstanding debts	+	
	Assets subtotal		
From this page:	Less: Other debts	–	
	Your net worth is:		

Source: Richard E. Mayer

"For a lot of small newspapers, three dollars a week is quite a bit of money," said Miller, who started selling the column in March 2002. "Some of them are barely scraping by. I don't charge much because I want to reach a lot of people."

The column, at five hundred words, usually consists of a reader's question on an issue affecting older Americans and Miller's answer. Chatty and very informative, each column invites readers to submit questions by e-mail or regular mail. "Great idea!" he tells a reader who says her husband has been "spending too darn much time around the house" and is looking for a way for both of them to do volunteer work. Readers are directed to his free Web site (www.savvysenior.org), where they can also submit questions, read recent columns, and find links to other helpful sites for older people. He receives up to thirty questions a week, he said, many dealing with Social Security or Medicare. He responds to each. "I either answer their questions or tell them where they can get answers," he said.

The four hundred papers that run his column have a combined circulation of 4 million with a potential 12 million readers. The biggest is the *Las Vegas Review-Journal*, which has a daily circulation of 170,000 and a Sunday circulation of 225,000; the smallest are some rural weekly papers with circulations of less than 1,000, like the *Forum* in Floodwood, Minnesota, and the *County Line* in Eskridge, Kansas. Despite the column's tiny price, Miller said he made about $40,000 a year after expenses and before taxes.

He started writing a column about older people three years ago after his mother and father died within three weeks of each other. "That really shook me up," he said. "So I got involved with older people at a retirement community here in Norman. I thought it would help me get through the grieving process." The column was first published free in the *Norman Transcript*, which has a daily circulation of about 16,500. Soon, other papers in the area expressed an interest.

Miller decided to try selling the column around the country. He sent letters and sample columns to sixty-two hundred of the roughly twelve thousand daily and weekly papers in the United States. One of those who responded was Raymond Linex II, the editor of the *Corsicana Daily Sun* in Corsicana, Texas. His paper runs the column every Wednesday, and he says it is popular with his town's large number of older people. But Linex said the deciding factor was the price. "We wouldn't have been able to run the column if it hadn't been so affordable for us," he added. "We're in a very tight ad market and have lost a Kmart retail store and a Kmart distribution center, which employed four hundred people." Linex said his paper planned to stick with "The Savvy Senior." "We have a need for that kind of column because there's nobody on our staff who can write it," he said. "And the price is just perfect for us."

Patricia St. Louis, the managing editor of the *Fountain Valley News*, a weekly newspaper in Fountain, Colorado, also bought the column. She praises it for the help it provides readers on issues like Medicare. She described it as a "good, important column that is full of information and resources. But I jumped on it because of the price," she added. "It's worth four or five times that."

Miller said he wanted to continue selling his column to newspapers but was exploring financial backing for his Web site from a nonprofit group. "I want to provide a service for seniors," he said. "I started the column with the idea of helping older people. I like older people and always have. Doing this column is gratifying. People are always grateful, because a lot of them just don't know where to turn. A lot of stuff we take for granted can be very complicated to older people. There's so much information for them to deal with. Many times they hear about something on television and have questions about it."

Miller is a native of Independence, Kansas, and has an undergraduate degree in education from Kansas State University and a graduate degree in education from Wichita State University. He worked for eight years in operations and events for the University of Oklahoma's athletic department in Norman before turning to his column. He is the stadium announcer for the university's football and basketball games—which he describes as a "part-time hobby job"—and was the announcer for gymnastics at the 1996 Summer Olympic Games in Atlanta.

"I started 'The Savvy Senior' for fun," he said. "But a lot of people have responded to it. It's amazing how many seniors are isolated and don't know where to turn for help."

resources

ON THE WEB

www.aarp.org/revmort is the AARP Web site for just about everything you might want to know about reverse mortgages.

www.BestPlaces.net is one of the best Internet sites for retirement planning. It allows you to compare not only cost-of-living data, but information on housing, crime, education, economics, health, and climate.

It also has a calculator that allows you to figure how much income you would need to maintain your current lifestyle in another city or region. Another section of the site allows you to list your preferences for the above categories; it will then produce a list of cities that match your description of what you are looking for in a place to live.

www.Bloomberg.com has some good "what if" calculators that allow you to see, among other things, the advantages of prepaying a mortgage. The site is operated by Bloomberg News.

www.cepr.net is the Web site of the Center for Economic Policy Research in Washington. It has a lot of good data relevant to the Social Security debate.

www.the-dma.org/consumers is the site of the Direct Marketing Association. It allows you to remove your name from its members' mailing lists.

www.ehealthinsurance.com is excellent for health insurance information and for purchasing individual policies.

www.grandmabetty.com is a quirky but interesting site operated by Betty Fox, a grandmother in Queens. It offers a little bit of everything, including some good links to other sites as well as information on how to stretch your dollars and get free products.

www.kff.org is run by the Kaiser Family Foundation and provides comprehensive health-care data on the states. The site was primarily designed for health policy researchers and policy makers, according to Larry Levitt, vice president of the foundation. "But now we find that everyday consumers are using it as well," he said.

No wonder. By clicking on "state health facts" on the home page of this well-designed site you can, for instance, learn which states have a prescription drug program for the elderly, where Medicare health maintenance organizations are most available, and the average price of prescriptions in the various states. The states are also ranked in various categories and compared with national averages; color-coded maps provide visual comparisons.

Take the price of drugs, for example. In 2001 the national average cost of a single prescription was $49.84. However, that same prescription could run from as little as $41.25 in Alabama to as much as $59.83 in Alaska. New York ranked fourth highest at $58.44. New Jersey was second at $59.18, and Connecticut came in ninth at $52.93. California was no. 22, at $48.62; Illinois came in at no. 18 at $49.36; and Texas ranked no. 12 at $50.84.

"The differences among states is striking," Levitt said. "And a lot of the differences are regional; it's cheaper in the South than in the Northeast."

www.mathsisfun.com is for people who can't remember the finer points of high school or college math or are trying to come to grips with math terms that often appear in financial data and articles.

www.movinon.net is popular with retirees interested in traveling in a recreational vehicle.

www.nahu.org is run by the National Association of Health Underwriters and can help you find an independent insurance broker in your area.

www.ofheo.gov is the Web site of the Office of Federal Housing Enterprise Oversight, a government agency that tracks changes in home values.

www.phrma.org is operated by the Pharmaceutical Research and Manufacturers of America. It is an excellent source of information on free prescription medicines from drug companies.

www.practicalmoneyskills.com is a really good site for basic help on personal finances.

www.Realtor.com is a great site for looking at homes for sale around the country. It's operated by the National Association of Realtors.

www.RetirementLiving.com is best at comparing the taxes imposed by each state. It also has links to news sources and publications about seniors and retirement. There is a directory of state agencies that deal with issues of aging, and visitors to the site can sign up for a free e-mail newsletter.

The site also has sections on retirement communities and senior housing, as well as products and services. One warning: those offering housing, services, and products have not been evaluated by the site; they are simply there because they have paid a fee.

www.savvysenior.org is the Web site of Jim Miller, whose column called "The Savvy Senior" runs in more than four hundred small daily and weekly newspapers around the country. You can read recent columns and send Miller questions through the site.

www.ssa.gov is the Web site operated by the Social Security Administration. It provides an enormous amount of information on rules and benefits. Its data are rock-solid and accepted by all sides in the political debate over Social Security's future. You can use the site to request an estimate of your benefits, or you can calculate your own. This latter feature is important to early retirees, because it allows them to find out exactly how much their benefits will be reduced if they retire prior to age sixty-two and have several years of reduced income that becomes part of their benefits calculation.

www.smartmoney.com, operated by *Smart Money* magazine, is helpful with real estate and other financial issues.

www.taxfoundation.org is a good source of information on property taxes.

www.2young2retire.com is a fascinating site for retirees and those with aspirations to retire. It is operated by Howard and Marika Stone of Weehawken, New Jersey. Among other things, the site contains stories about people who, instead of accepting traditional retirement, have made transitions to new and what they consider more interesting careers and lifestyles. The Goldens, the couple in chapter 4 who spent time on the road in a motor home before settling down, were first featured here.

The Web site is the Stones' equivalent of the Goldens' Winnebago. Howard, sixty-eight, left a marketing career at a publisher, while Marika, sixty-two, is a former freelance business writer who now teaches yoga. Howard said: "I was tired of the pace of business and all that business travel, but the idea of retirement didn't really appeal to me. At the same time, I wanted to be involved in something that would make a difference. I think the Web site has turned out to be a help to people, because it tells stories that relate to their changing concerns and aspirations."

The Stones have also published a book, *Too Young to Retire: An Off-the-Road Map for the Rest of Your Life* (Writers' Collective, 2003), which can be ordered from their Web site.

OFF THE SHELF

Generations: The History of America's Future, 1584 to 2069 (William Morrow, 1992), by William Strauss and Neil Howe, is *the* book to read for understanding generational issues and how they play out in our history and public policy.

The Great 401(k) Hoax: Why Your Family's Financial Security Is at Risk and What You Can Do About It (Perseus Publishing, 2002), by William Wolman and Anne Colamosca, is a scathing attack on the idea, much ballyhooed by Wall Street, that 401(k) plans linking workers' retirement well-being to the stock market are an easy way to amass wealth.

The authors remind us that these so-called defined-contribution plans were created to replace traditional defined-benefit pension plans not to empower or enrich workers but to relieve corporations of the expense and responsibility of funding and maintaining traditional pensions that are protected and guaranteed under federal law.

Companies may or may not match employee 401(k) contributions, but to the extent they do so with company stock it's even cheaper— never mind the financial risk to employees (remember Enron). This means that when employees retire, they take their 401(k) money and that's that. A company has no pesky long-term commitments to retirees. All this is great for the corporate bottom line.

But is it good for workers? Not necessarily, Wolman and Colamosca argue, especially for those at the lower end of the salary scale. They point out that, according to the Employment Benefit Research Institute, the average 401(k) account shrank to $49,024 in 2000 from $55,502 in 1999. But they say these figures look better than things really are, since the averages include the 401(k) plans of top earners. They contend a more realistic figure is the median 401(k) account, with half above and half below. That figure was $13,493 in 2000, down from $15,246 in 1999. These numbers do not point to fat retirement years.

In the end, the authors say, many lower-paid workers are simply not able to save enough in 401(k) plans to give them sufficient money in retirement, especially if the stock market is in a long slump. Privatizing Social Security would make things even worse, they assert, turning a sure thing into a stock market bet. The authors project that stock returns during the next two decades, adjusted for inflation, will be just 1.9 percent.

"Our analysis strongly suggests that the great bull market that saw the Dow Jones Industrial Average quintuple between the end of the Cold War in the summer of 1989 and mid-July 1999 will be followed by a stock market slump that could last for two decades and could financially devastate the unprepared family," the authors write. "This is what history suggests."

What do they think we should do? For starters, they call for workers to have unrestricted investment choices for their 401(k) plans. They also think company matches should be in cold cash, not stock. They urge workers to shift investment to fixed-income securities.

Longevity Revolution: As Boomers Become Elders (Berkeley Hills Books, 2001), by Theodore Roszak, is an excellent antidote to the gloom-and-doom many writers and commentators associate with the graying of America. Roszak sees the aging population as a reason to celebrate, not worry; he sees opportunity where some others see disaster.

Retire in Style: 50 Affordable Places Across America (Next Decade, 2001), by Warren R. Bland, provides economic and lifestyle information on the author's choices of good retirement spots. He gives numerical rankings to his selections, with the highest score being 60. The scores are based on a number of categories, including quality of life, cost of living, health care, transportation, and cultural activities.

Boulder, Colorado, finished at the top of the list with 52 points. It scored especially high on quality of life and recreational activities. But it only had a fair rating for cost of living, which is about 20 percent above the national average; housing costs are about 60 percent above the average.

The other cities in the top twelve, all of which scored at least 48 points, were Portland, Oregon; Asheville, North Carolina; Austin, Texas; San Antonio, Texas; Chapel Hill, North Carolina; Colorado Springs, Colorado; Eugene, Oregon; Fayetteville, Arkansas; Fort Collins, Colorado; Gainesville, Florida; and Medford/Ashland, Oregon.

Retirement Bible (John Wiley, 2001), by Lynn O'Shaughnessy, can help you get a grip on your financial situation, a move vital to retirement planning. Published by the same company that does the "Dummies" series of how-to books, it's comprehensive and easy to understand.

Retirement on a Shoestring (4th edition, Globe Pequot Press, 2002), by John Howells, is filled with strategies for making your retirement money go as far as possible. It is written for people who don't have plump pensions or 401(k) plans and may have to live pretty much off Social Security. It gives down-to-earth advice on cutting expenses and looks beyond the "best places" often cited in books and magazine articles to even cheaper, but acceptable, towns and areas. It covers topics from medical insurance and expenses to the pros and cons of retiring to less expensive areas overseas.

Social Security: The Phony Crisis (University of Chicago Press, 2001), by Dean Baker and Mark Weisbrot, is a valuable guide for anyone who is nervous or confused over the political discourse about the future of Social Security. The authors, both liberal economists, argue convincingly that because of overly conservative economic projections, Social Security is not in danger and doesn't need to be saved by putting some of its funds into individual stock market accounts, as President Bush and many conservatives advocate. They see the drive to privatize Social Security as coming from ideologues who have never liked the system and would like to diminish or destroy it, as well as from Wall Street brokerage firms eager for the huge commissions such stock accounts would generate.

Take Control with Your 401(k): An Employee's Guide to Maximizing Your Investments (Dearborn Trade Publishing, 2002), by David L. Wray, does not take issue with the 401(k) concept. After all, the author is president of the Profit Sharing/401(k) Council of America. But it does offer practical advice for managing your 401(k) retirement account and exercising your options. From opening an account to cashing out, the details, rules, and terms are clearly explained.

index

about the author

FRED BROCK is a business editor and writes the "Seniority" column for the *New York Times*. He has also worked for the *Wall Street Journal, Houston Chronicle*, and *Louisville Courier-Journal*. He lives in New Jersey.